Himself

# Robert Benchley

## HIS LIFE AND GOOD TIMES

by Babette
Rosmond

1970

DOUBLEDAY & COMPANY, INC., GARDEN CITY, NEW YORK

## ACKNOWLEDGMENTS

It's not possible to convey proper thanks to Mrs. Robert Benchley; without her generous, enthusiastic help there would simply have been no book. I am also deeply indebted to Nathaniel Benchley and Robert Benchley, Jr., for their interest and kindness.

Among the friends of Robert Benchley who have freely shared their recollections I am particularly grateful to:

| | | |
|---|---|---|
| Marc Connelly | John Hay Whitney | Howard Dietz |
| Del Sharbutt | Betty Starbuck | Ann Honeycutt |
| Edith Meiser | Patricia Collinge | Charlie Berns |
| Beatrice Ames | Donald Ogden Stewart | Tony Soma |
| H. C. Potter | Maxwell Kriendler | Hobart Weeks |

Whatever it was that made Robert Benchley so very special tended to rub off a bit on those who were close to him.

B.R.

# CONTENTS

## INTRODUCTION

On a cold, sunny February morning I drove to Scarsdale to spend the day with Mrs. Robert Benchley. She was standing outside her house talking to a neighbor who had pulled up to the curb; she concluded her chat when she saw me, and waved. "Pull forward a little," she said. "Were my directions all right?" She had drawn an excellent map, and I told her so.

We entered the house that the Benchleys had bought in 1920. It was immaculate and attractive with various periods of furniture. The intangible atmosphere that evokes instant reaction to houses worked positively: this was a comfortable one.

"This room is devoted to Bob's things," said Mrs. Benchley, showing me a sunny, booklined study. It was indeed, but so was the rest of the house. In every room and along the staircase were framed photographs and original drawings that had played some part in the Benchley career. When we finished a short tour, Mrs.

Benchley took out a huge scrapbook and said, "There. Do your homework."

The scrapbook contained literally hundreds of clippings of obituaries, as well as commendations from the War Department, letters from strangers and notes from close friends.

"One letter came from somebody I didn't know at all," said Mrs. Benchley. "It was from a man who had asked Bob for fifty dollars. Bob sent him a quart of whiskey with five ten dollar bills wrapped around it, and a note saying, 'There's a five-cent rebate on the bottle.'

"Then there was the time he was here with us during the week before Christmas. Two policemen rang the doorbell and came in and started to talk . . . hands out, naturally. Well, Bob signaled to me that he only had a ten on him and would I please go upstairs and see if I had a five . . . I went up, but by the time I got back they had run out of conversation and he had given them the ten . . . but I didn't realize it and gave them my five as well."

I began to take notes from the scrapbook, which was the purpose of my visit. Mrs. Benchley made frequent comments as I turned the pages.

Now eighty, she is a small, trim, pretty woman with blue eyes, clear skin and a brisk way of speaking.

She pointed to a little diamond pin she was wearing, shaped into the number "29" with a bar underneath. "I saw you looking at that. Bob gave it to me on our 30th anniversary—but he didn't dare put '30' down because you know, that's what newspapermen do when they mean something is finished. So it's 29—with a service stripe underneath!"

We began to talk about her husband and I mentioned that one of the difficulties with writing a book about him was the danger of oversentimentalizing. Mrs. Benchley nodded. "Bob never refused anyone *any*thing.

"People don't realize how much time Bob spent here. He hated the country, and when he was in the Music Box Revue, doing the Treasurer's Report, he had arthritis so badly he had to leave his crutches in the wings. Doctor told him he absolutely couldn't commute, so he took the place in town. People asked me if we were going to be divorced . . . how absurd! Except for the times he was in Hollywood he called me once, sometimes twice a day—he had to be in New York covering theater, and he just didn't like Scarsdale. It was too much for him to make the trip every night. Do you know, in all the years we were married we never had a cross word? Well, just once. That was a phone call . . . he liked Franklin Roosevelt and I didn't, and we argued about that, and finally I said, 'Oh, you're right, you're always right,' and Bob said, 'That's a coward's answer.' But that was the only time."

Some time past noon I was offered a drink, and we stopped working for a while. Mrs. Benchley had written me, "I'm no cook, but I can offer you a respectable salad." Lunch was not only respectable but memorable: crabmeat-and-egg with a special dressing.

The dining room was bright and large, ornamented
with cabinets filled with precious china. I was shown
some plates that had come over on the *Mayflower*, and
was told stories about other pieces that had been used by
generations of Darlings, Mrs. Benchley being Gertrude
Darling Benchley.

We talked about some of the famous contemporaries
of Robert Benchley. I knew that Donald Ogden Stewart
had been the first person to offer alcoholic refreshment
to Benchley. ("We were both White Ribboners then,"
said Mrs. B.) I asked about Stewart and Mrs. Benchley
frowned.

"Well, he was often irritating. When Bob was in the
hospital Donald phoned and spoke to me there and
said, 'Have a nurse call me every hour to report,' and I
just told him the nurses were there to take care of Bob,
not to telephone *him*. He owed Bob two thousand
dollars for a long time, and finally paid it back in the
form of a man's fur coat. Bob wore the coat twice—
and caught cold each time, so he gave the thing to me."

Mrs. Benchley told about summers at Antibes with
the Gerald Murphys. "They were so graceful and beautiful. And so tragic. Their only son caught T.B.—he
had just had a tonsillectomy and was being carried by
their chauffeur, who was a consumptive. The chauffeur
coughed right in the child's face, and after that operation—well, they lost him.

"Zelda Fitzgerald was so lovely—and such a marvelous dancer. She was taking a ballet class then, and
wanted me to drive her to Paris. '*You*'re the sober one,'

she'd say. Dottie Parker was so anxious that summer to have her breasts operated on, to make them smaller, but I don't know if she did or not."

I mentioned that Nathaniel Benchley had indicated something less than kindness on the part of Mrs. Parker when he was collecting material for his biography of his father published in 1955.

"She wasn't a very nice person—well, no. I won't say that. Whenever she came up here, she never helped with the dishes—fled upstairs. But she was fun. First time in New York—Bob and I had a tiny apartment on 23rd Street, right under the El, and we were visiting Neysa McMein in her little studio—it was dark—Dottie realized I was fresh from the country and had never used make-up. 'Have some powder on your nose,' she said, handing me a compact. Well, it turned out to be rouge."

"That's not so funny," I said.

"When Bob died and Dottie heard about his death she said, 'That's dandy!' "

"Oh, maybe that was the way you say 'oh great' when something really horrible happens. . . ."

My hostess nodded briefly. "She *was* funny. I was right there, the time in the Algonquin, when some little chorus girl and Dottie were going into the dining room and the girl stepped back and said, 'Age before beauty' and Dottie said very quickly, 'Pearls before swine.' I was right there when she said it.

"She dedicated one of her books 'to John,' but by the time the book came out it was quite another John!

Lucky it was a common name like that. She was devoted
to Eddie Parker, though. I don't remember why they
were divorced. He came from a Hartford family, they
had a big sporting goods store. Yes, she *was* fond of him.
But so many after that. . . . She was a pretty woman, I
suppose, with that dark hair and great big eyes, but so—
so *misshapen*, really."

"I liked Minna, F.P.A.'s first wife. She was so nice. So
was he. They all were. Dottie used to get involved with
a lot of them. She was mad for Deems Taylor. *And* for
Charles MacArthur. You know, they all had these
pseudonyms when they wrote for the Conning Tower.
Deems Taylor was Smeed—that's Deems backwards—
and Howard Dietz was Freckles, and—"

"Wasn't Edna Millay signing herself Nancy Boyd?"

"Oh, maybe. There were the Brouns, or, rather, Heywood and Ruth Hale. She was president of the Lucy
Stone League and always called herself Ruth Hale.
Once she said to Bob, 'I have never demanded faithful-
ness from Heywood and he has never demanded it from
me.' Bob said, 'He didn't have to worry'; but of course
I never told her that."

Mrs. Benchley sprang up to attend to the coffee.

"Edna Ferber was very funny. Woollcott was rude
as could be. Once there was this friend of ours who
was longing to meet him. Bob and I were standing with
Alec outside the Rose Room at the Algonquin and along
came this girl, and I told Alec how anxious she was. He
waited until she was within earshot and then he said,

'And now, Bob, I leave you to your uninteresting friends.'"

She reflected a moment. "But that wasn't the way he was as a rule."

We talked about some of the people connected with *The New Yorker* in the twenties and thirties as we drank excellent coffee.

"Bob enjoyed Wolcott Gibbs and his wife a lot. Shortly before Bob died they were having lunch together, I wasn't there, and they were talking about front false teeth, you know—whether you'd have a big gold one right in front, and Mrs. Gibbs said she wanted an emerald tooth! Well, Bob remembered that, and he saw a little emerald and had it mounted—couldn't do it as a tooth, of course, but made it into a ring. He died around that time . . . so I paid for it."

Mrs. Benchley wouldn't let me help her clear away the luncheon things—although I remembered what she'd said about Mrs. Parker and made efforts to do so—and I went back to my notes from the scrapbooks in the living room.

Later on, we walked through the house again, looking at pictures. On a wall was a framed drawing of Bob's famous room at the Royalton.

"Oh, I remember that," I said.

Mrs. Benchley was aware that I had known her husband many years before. "How was that," she asked.

I told her about meeting him just before World War II, how, after a dull Sunday afternoon at a football game, my date had turned out to be a friend of a friend

of Benchley. The gray day had been turned into gold,
leading to a brief friendship with Benchley that influenced my entire life. It was hard to say this in a few
words, and I concluded,

"... I was just eighteen."

Mrs. Benchley smiled. "That didn't do any harm, did
it?" she said.

# ROBERT BENCHLEY

HIS LIFE AND GOOD TIMES

**NOTE**

Illustrations may be found
following pages 72, 120, 168.

CHAPTER ONE

# "The Smells
# of Saturday"

"Robert Charles Benchley, born Isle of Wight, September 15, 1807. Shipped as cabin boy on the *Florence J. Marble*, 1815. Arrested for bigamy and murder in Port Said 1817. Released 1820. Wrote *Tale of Two Cities*. Married Princess Anastasia of Portugal 1831. Children: Prince Rupprecht and several little girls. Wrote *Uncle Tom's Cabin* 1850. Editor of *Godeys Ladies Book* 1851–1856. Began *Les Miserables* in 1870, finished by Victor Hugo. Died 1871. Buried in Westminster Abbey."

This succinct account of a man's life is colorful, impressive and a black lie. Benchley wrote it to please himself and foil biographers. He could no more have written a straight autobiographical essay than he could have swum the English channel. Too much fact tended to bore him; he came from a race rich in imagination, a people inclined to be more than a little fey. "It is too late to do anything about it now, but I sometimes wish that my paternal ancestors had not been Welsh." Robert Benchley once wrote, "I can't seem to get the hang of Welsh songs."

The first Benchley in Worcester, Massachusetts, was Henry W. Benchley, whose ancestors had come to this country from Merthyr Tydfil, Glamorgan, Wales, some years before the American Revolution. Henry had been in politics and became Lieutenant Governor of Massachusetts from 1856 to 1858. He went to Texas to set up a station for the Underground Railroad, helping slaves escape to the North. He was caught and convicted and eventually housed for a short time in a Texas jail.

One of Benchley's ancestors fought in the American Revolution. His mother's family was from Protestant Northern Ireland, and in later years Benchley often said that he stayed in the house every St. Patrick's Day. As an Orangeman, he was afraid of being stoned to death.

Maria Jane Moran, Benchley's mother, a strong-minded woman, married Charlie Benchley in 1874. Their first son, Edmund Nathaniel, born in 1876, was one of the blessed: handsome, brilliant, humorous, and with an aptitude for dramatics. Maria Jane, who was called Jennie, adored him.

September 15, 1889, was the time to be born for Robert Charles Benchley. It was a rather unexpected event; Edmund was just about to enter high school, and another baby had not been planned. But Edmund was so pleased with the new arrival that he carried Robert in his arms about the house, took long walks with him, and saw to it that Robert got more than his share of familial attention. The Benchley boys loved each other, and Robert leaned toward hero-worship of Edmund all through his Worcester days.

Worcester in the 1890s was bustling, thriving, and taking quite seriously its own municipal motto, "Heart of the Commonwealth." It was riding a tide of prosperity based on textiles and the manufacture of machinery, such as the first workable gadget for folding envelopes. The affluence was reflected on Worcester's tree-lined residential streets—dwellings topped with cupolas and mansard roofs. The well-kept lawns were decorated with octagonal summerhouses and cast-iron deer. The cupolas were crowned with tiaras of iron lacework, and the houses radiated rectitude, which was the cement of social and commercial life in that well-to-do New England town. The city was surrounded by hills and little valleys dotted with ponds, and on Sundays in winter the Worcester folk went out driving in a kind of sleigh known as a pung.

The Worcester Art Museum was founded in 1896 and in 1898 a City Hall in Italian Renaissance style was built. Worcester residents had been long accustomed to the best in theater and concert stage. They had seen Bernhardt, Jenny Lind, Fanny Kemble, and had been addressed by Abraham Lincoln, Matthew Arnold, John

Brown, and Thoreau. There was a music festival every
year, beginning in 1859.

Robert Benchley saw his first show at the Worcester
Theater, where it is likely another illustrious Worcester
boy attended: S. N. Behrman. Benchley's first play was
*Jack and the Beanstalk*, staged by Mr. Ben Teal, with
the Eight Pretty Maids, the Ten Good Fairies and "some
of the Forty Thieves."

Benchley mentioned seeing, on the Worcester Common, in 1893, his first giraffe. As he put it, "A giraffe
is not an animal that one sees for the first time without looking twice. A giraffe, no matter how you look
at it, is out of the ordinary. Of course, I was only three
years old at the time but a child three years old has
ears . . . I always knew that my father was a phlegmatic man, but I didn't realize that he was as phlegmatic
as not to tell us that there was a giraffe on Worcester
Common. Why wasn't I taken down to see it? I was
taken to watch fireworks on the Fourth of July, and
hated it. I was taken to the circus, and all that the circus
had to offer was some old elephants and tigers that
everybody had seen before. But they held out on me
when a real attraction came to town. Maybe they
thought it would be over my head, and so help me I
didn't mean to write it that way. (However, you notice
I'm letting it stand.)"

"And I remember being taken to a Fourth of July
fireworks exhibition, at which I became so terrified that
I tried to crawl under the seats, and slipped down
between the boards of the bleacher flooring. Just my

hands and arms slipped down, but I caught my chin a nasty crack, and several dozen people had to get up in order to extricate me. I was furious, and to this episode I attribute my subsequent hatred of explosives and war."

It was no joke, that hatred of war. Pacifism played an important part in Benchley's later life. He may have hated the fireworks when he was a child (Jennie hated them, too, and was never afraid to voice her opinions), but he was to become more articulate about his feelings during World Wars I and II.

When Robert was just six, in 1895, he was sent to kindergarten. He was a thin child, blue-eyed, with light brown hair and a rather wistful expression. He coughed a great deal; his teacher suspected him of being tubercular. Actually, he had recovered from an anonymous attack of whooping cough: Jennie didn't recognize any such infirmity in her child. He says that on the first day of school a little girl pulled his chair out from under him. It wasn't a very big chair but his pride was hurt and he went directly home. To make things worse, his mother took him right back to school where he was given "something worsted" and told to sew a beaver on a card.

Benchley's older brother, Edmund, had taught him a poem, which Benchley says is one of the few he had never forgotten. He recited it in kindergarten that morning. It went:

> *My mother-in-law has lately died,*
> *For her my heart doth yearn;*
> *I know she's with the angels now,*
> *For she was too tough to burn.*

after which Benchley made his little kindergarten bow and marched home again. Memories of that kind of recitation, and his exposure to Jennie's hatred of the Spanish-American War, always kept him from joining in so-called Gay Nineties songfests: barbershop harmony for "She's Only a Bird in a Gilded Cage," "The Curse of an Aching Heart," "Sweet Adeline" and other sentimental ballads. He said he'd sing anything that came out of the 1900s but left the '90s to be celebrated by others fortunate enough to have been born after the turn of the century.

Benchley's musical education wasn't much more fruitful than his kindergarten experiences. The first instrument that he "took lessons on" was the banjo. It was "not the little, short-necked, combination banjo and mandolin of today, but the original Negro instrument with the long neck and five strings, one of which was always broken."

In those days there was no such thing as walking into a music store and buying a banjo part for the latest popular tune. You had to wait until somebody called "The Banjo King" had made a special arrangement in five flats, and as "The Banjo King" never got around to his arranging until two or three years after a number had died down, the result was that I had nothing to play but "The Return of the Jolly Haymakers" and the "Cream City Patrol."

Benchley's sessions at grammar school (Hard Knocks —1908), as he called it, began at nine in the morning and let out at 3 P.M. The children were on their own from that time on, and Benchley points out that in those days there were no streamlined roadsters, no personal planes, no movie palaces and so on, but he says that these deprivations gave him something that stood him well in after life. It made a man of him.

In fact, when school was out in Worcester, the children often hitched rides on the back of ice wagons, which Benchley says toughens a boy's stomach muscles and teaches him to like ice.

Young Benchley rode a bicycle—sometimes twenty-five times around a vacant lot, ringing the bell the whole time.

Saturdays were different. Benchley once wrote a piece about the smells of childhood, and he was particularly caught up with the smells of Saturday. He claimed the smells started on Friday evening, when the bread was set on the kitchen table and the beans put to soak nearby. "The smell of the cold bread-dough when the napkins were lifted from the pans always meant no school tomorrow, and was a preliminary to the no school today smells of Saturday, which began to permeate the kitchen quite early. As the kitchen was the sole port of entry and exit during the morning's play outside, they became inextricably mixed up with not only cooking, but "duck-on-the-rock," "Indian guide," and that informal scrimmaging in which boys become engaged in backyards which goes by the name of either football or baseball according to the season.

"In New England, of course, the *leit motif* among the Saturday smells was the one of beans baking, but

bread and pies ran at a close second. A good cake in
the oven could hold its own too. Then, along about
11:30 the Saturday noon dinners began to loom up,
being usually more plebian than the Sunday noon dinner,
it took the combined form of cabbage, turnips, beets,
and corned beef, all working together in one pot with
the potatoes to make the famous New England boiled
dinner."

Benchley says that, in New England, what was known
as the heavy meal came in the middle of the day and
anyone who asked you to "dinner" at supper-time would
wear lorgnettes.

Worcester had its share of food stores including the
E. S. Pierce Company (not Boston's S. S. Pierce), and
there was the Boston Fish and Oyster House, B. J.
Bertels and Caesar Misch & Co. where you could get
clothing on credit. But Benchley was more interested in
candy stores.

There were two distinct brands of candy in those
days in Worcester: the candy one could buy in the
drugstore on Sunday, and the weekday brand which,
according to Benchley and also according to present
day standards of pure food, should have "set up a bright
green fermentation with electric lights" in one's stomach.
The drugstore candy was only had for lack of something better, but on weekdays came the real orgies.
There was a candy store run by an old lady who,
Benchley claimed, was an agent in the employ of the
German government in a farsighted scheme to unfit the
American people for participation in the war which was

to come. The arrival of children in this store would be heralded by the jangle of a little bell, which was followed by a long period of concentration while the small customer made up his mind which of the candies he was going to buy. Benchley says, "In this collection of tasty morsels, the one which haunts my memory most insistently is a confection called the wine cup, a cone-shaped bit of colored sugar filled with some villainous fluid which, when bitten, ran down over the chin and on to the necktie. It was capped by a dingy piece of marshmallow which was supposed to be removed with the teeth before drinking the ambrosia within, but usually at the first nibble the whole structure collapsed with the result that inveterate wine cup consumers had a telltale coating of sugared water down the front of the coat, and, on a cold day, a slight glaze of ice on the chin. What went on in the stomach no one knows, but it does not make a very pretty picture."

In later years Benchley tended to blame one of his endearing shortcomings (he said a list of these would be furnished upon application to any one of his friends) on a bad fairy who seemed to have endowed him at birth with a paucity of visual imagination—amounting practically to a squint. Or so he said.

He blames the limitation on the street scenes in Worcester, claiming it was not the ideal locale for the *Chanson de Roland* or the *Adventures of Ivanhoe*. It didn't have quite the atmosphere essential to a complete feeling for the Wessex of Hardy, and . . . "it is not

likely that Hugo had any such place in mind when he
wrote *Les Miserables*. However, regardless of what
Hugo had in mind, *I* have Front Street, Worcester, in
mind when I read it."

Edmund graduated from high school in 1894 and
applied for and received an appointment to the Military
Academy at West Point. Visitors from Worcester would
occasionally swarm to West Point: Charlie, Jennie,
Robert, Jennie's sister, Aunt Lizzie, and her daughter,
Maybelle. They all loved it: the grim gray Palisades,
the line of marching cadets and the ceremonies. Particularly Jennie.

Robert was a little frightened of the sunset gun and
whenever it was about to be fired, he would dart away
from Jennie and try to hide someplace.

Edmund's last year at West Point was, unluckily,
1898, the year of the Spanish-American War. His class
was graduated early in order to go on active duty in
Cuba. Edmund chose the Infantry and was given a
three-day leave at home before being shipped out. He
left for Cuba in June 1898.

The Fourth of July celebration in Worcester that
year was a shattering one for the Benchleys and in a
large measure accounts for Robert's lifelong hatred of
the occasion. Firecrackers were the real thing in those
days; the smoke of the gunpowder clung to the grass
and the smell hung in the air for hours. This was New
England at the time of America's version of *la belle
epoque*—comfortable, middle-class life in placid small
towns—there has never been anything like it before or

since for a sense of security, whether false or true. July 4, 1898, was a hot and muggy day. Robert hated the big firecrackers, but his father, Charlie, took him on the lawn and let him fool around with some toy torpedoes.

As Robert played, Jennie watched from her rocking chair on the porch. A man with a newspaper in his pocket approached the house. The Benchleys had never seen the man before; he turned out to be a reporter for the *Worcester Spy*, and he had come to tell them that Edmund had been killed in Cuba on July 1.

Jennie's reaction to the news of Edmund's death was terrifying. Her anger and shock temporarily robbed her of reason. She said clearly, "Oh, why couldn't it have been Robert?" And through the relentless, all-powerful grapevine that springs to life in times of drama, Jennie's phrase became semipublic property in Worcester.

In the late 1930s, one of Benchley's favorite novels was Evelyn Waugh's *Handful of Dust*, which contains one of the most soul-searing scenes in modern literature. The heroine, Brenda Last, who has been having an affair with a man named John Beaver, is told "John is dead." For a second she thinks it is Beaver who is being discussed, then she realizes it is her small son, John, who has been killed. Her first words are, "Thank God."

Whenever Benchley tried to guide the reading habits of young friends, this book was at the top of his recommendations. Certainly Jennie's words on that Fourth of July must have haunted Robert all his life, but they did not appear to blight what was otherwise a very happy childhood, for Jennie spent the rest of Robert's years at home making up for her words. She did literally everything for her only remaining son. Once when Robert's Sunday school teacher complained about him, Jennie yelled at her. "Don't you ever do anything to interfere with Robert's sense of humor!" What Robert had done was to change the word of a hymn from "Mercy drops around us are falling" to "Lemon drops around us are falling."

Jennie Benchley had always disapproved of war, but the death of her adored elder son made her a fanatic pacifist. There is a Benchley legend about Jennie trying to get a passport many years later and having to think twice when it came to answering the question, "Do you swear to defend the Constitution of the United States against all enemies, domestic and foreign?" Jennie asked if she *had* to swear this, was told she did; replied, "Well, there are days when I wouldn't." (But she did get her passport.)

She also banned all guns, swords and firecrackers from her house, and her horror of Fourth of July celebrations stayed with Robert forever, as even his lighthearted pieces often indicated.

Robert's father, Charlie, was a mayor's clerk in Worcester for thirty years. He wore pince-nez glasses, had a large moustache and was self-effacing to the point of invisibility. Benchley had a story that he used to tell about his father: Charlie had a watch given to him by a

grateful civic group, and every year he would touch
that watch to the mulberry bush outside the Worcester
House for luck for Harvard in the football games.

Charlie's chivalry was impressive, if occasionally ir-
relevant. One morning when Jennie was dressed for
church, her hat, which was secured with one of those
long gauzy veils of the period, caught fire as she bent
over the stove burner. The fire was soon put out but
Charlie said, "Oh, dear, that was my fault. I'm so sorry."

While he was growing up Benchley spent a good deal
in church listening to uplifting reformers at Christian
Endeavor every Sunday afternoon. It was at one of
these meetings that he heard Carry Nation preach about
the dangers of alcohol, and perhaps this was why for a
certain period of his life he was an ardent teetotaler.

Sometimes Robert attended these meetings with his
friend Gertrude Darling. They were schoolmates. They
had met in the third grade and Robert had already
announced to his peers and possible rivals that he intended to marry Gertrude, whose hair at that time was
still in braids.

The Benchley family was very much of a matriarchy.
Charlie was a nice, easy-going man, and Jennie was the
unquestioned head of the house. The person who played
the second most important part in the raising of Robert
Benchley was another strong-minded lady, Lillian Duryea, who had been engaged to Edmund and took an
active part in shaping the destiny of young Robert,
particularly so far as his schooling was concerned. This
may account for a habit of Robert's, much later on, of

using the name "Lillian" for any lady he was gently
poking fun at in print, even referring in one piece to a
mosquito as "Lillian."

Lillian in those days was a red-haired, handsome
creature, dominating to an almost monumental degree.
Spiritually, mentally, physically, she knew what she
wanted and couldn't imagine a situation in which she
wouldn't get it. For some reason, she had decided that
she was the proper person to run Robert's life, as she
had no doubt intended to run Edmund's.

When Robert was about ten, Lillian Duryea gave
him a Punch and Judy puppet set. This wasn't a toy—
the puppets were elegantly constructed. Bob learned
how to use them with great skill. Probably it was his
first chance to exploit the potential actor in him.

He would give his Punch and Judy shows at all
manner of parties, especially at church sociables, where
Gertrude Darling would applaud the actor and his
puppets. The Punch and Judy set and the screen behind
which the manipulator used to squat is still in existence,
mute testimony to Benchley's early interest in anything
theatrical.

Today Gertrude Benchley has made new costumes
for Punch, for Judy and for the Judge who sports black
satin britches and coat and a white ruffled shirt with
tiny, carefully marked stitches. Punch's nose is somewhat battered from the beatings he received from the
puppeteer (Benchley himself). It's hard to say which
looks more corrupt, the baby or the Judge . . .

Even as a child, Robert was an insatiable reader, a habit which he tried to share with others all his life. This may explain the fact that in the 1920s and 1930s several pretty young actresses showed up for work with stacks of literature. Such unexpected interests were, in many cases, largely due to the missionary zeal of Benchley, who insisted that reading was the supreme pleasure, and never, never an intellectual obligation.

During his boyhood, Robert began to develop a strong sense of social justice. Jennie would take him around at Christmas to visit a community center that cared for children less well off than he. Jennie may have ruled with a mailed fist, but she loved children and knew how much it meant to a child to be hurt—as Robert was one year when at one of the Christmas parties his present fell down from the tree and Santa never got around to reading his name.

It's undoubtedly a coincidence that Benchley as a grown man sometimes tended to accept Christmas with reservations. Some of his pieces dealt with a cross lady named Uncle Edith who would strike little children sitting at her feet as she told them ridiculous Christmas stories.

# CHAPTER TWO

# "There Is Such a Thing As Being a Studying Fool"

While Robert was growing up in the peaceful atmosphere of Worcester he behaved like most little boys. He liked to play more than he liked being in school, and the thorn in his life was dancing class. When he was little he used to feign measles and fallen arches on Saturday afternoons when the dreaded time came to put on the patent leather pumps. "After a Saturday morning of rolling around in the dirt and skinning kneecaps what red blooded man of ten or eleven would not rebel at being called in and given a hot bath in the middle of the day and crowded into a black suit merely to spend a sunny afternoon indoors with a bunch of girls in blue sashes." Benchley felt it was a wonder anybody ever got married after an experience

like that. As he put it, "I have braved the thin red line
of disapproving mothers seated along the wall at dancing
school. I have eluded the most eagle-eyed of hostesses
at young peoples' parties. I have definitely established
myself as a non-dancer in some of the dancingest circles
of my day. The only time that any celestial influence
gets me on my feet will be when it swoops me up for
good."

Strangely enough, one of Benchley's closest friends
later on in New York and Hollywood was Fred Astaire.
It is safe to assume Benchley never gave Astaire any
dancing lessons.

In 1907, when Robert was a junior in high school, the
strong-minded Lillian Duryea decided Robert needed a
better education than that provided by the Worcester
school system. She offered to stake him to a year at
Exeter and four years at whatever college he might
choose. Jennie didn't like the idea. She thought that
Robert could work his own way through and she didn't
want to be indebted to anybody. Lillian was perhaps
just a few filings more steely than Jennie, and Jennie
finally gave in—probably for the first time in her
history. But Jennie insisted the money was to be an out-
right gift rather than a loan which might prove a worri-
some burden to Robert.

That single year at Exeter taught Robert the joys of
all-male company. There wasn't one woman around,
and his discovery of youthful masculine horseplay was

an exciting one. His diary at the time mentions much
roughhousing with innocent and genuine pleasure:

Nov. 22, 1907:  Played football in the moonlight until
                nearly 11. Came back to the room and
                fooled around.
Jan. 21, 1908:  The room is on study-hours for rough-
                house last night.
Feb. 25, 1908:  Fat and I went to Town Hall and heard
                Jacob Riis lecture on "The Battle with
                the Slums." Very interesting.

The horseplay didn't interfere with Robert's studies
. . . he did well enough to make a couple of A's.

Lillian came to Boston often. Robert would meet her
and they would discuss his choice of college. He was
interested in Yale but Lillian was set on Harvard, and
Lillian was Lillian. She had had Edmund in her pocket;
now that he was dead, she apparently figured that
Robert might replace him as her consort (husband would
have been too mild a word for any mate of hers).
In spite of the difference in age—or maybe because of it,
since it made Robert that much easier to boss around—
Lillian had more than a friendly interest in her protégé's
career. This grew clear later on when Robert did marry
Gertrude Darling and was dropped by his protector
almost immediately. Lillian pretended Gertrude didn't
really exist: her plans had been upset and that wasn't
Duryea procedure.

When Robert graduated from Exeter he took entrance exams for Harvard, passed them, and spent

that summer at Lillian's home in Nyack, but before he
went off to Harvard, he made a point of seeing Gertrude, who was off for her freshman year at Smith. He
also signed an IOU to Lillian, promising to repay all
she spent on his education.

Jennie never did find out about this.

"My college education," wrote Robert Benchley,
"was no haphazard affair. My courses were all selected
with a very definite aim in view, with a serious purpose
in mind: No classes before 11 A.M. or after 2:30 P.M.
and nothing on Saturday. That was my slogan. On that
rock was my education built.

"As what is known as the Classical Course involved
practically no afternoon laboratory work, whereas in
the Scientific Course, a man's time was never his own
until 4 P.M. anyway, I went in for the Classics. But
only such Classics as allowed for a good sleep in the
morning. A man has his health to think of, there is
such a thing as being a studying fool.

"In my days (I was a classmate of the founder of the
college) a student could elect to take any courses in
the catalog, provided no two of his choices came at the
same hour. The only thing he was not supposed to mix
were scotch and gin.

"Under the elective system, my schedule was as
follows:

      Mondays, Wednesdays and Fridays at 11:
         Botany II-A
      Tuesdays and Thursdays at 11:
         English 26, The Social Life of Minor
         16th Century Poets

Mondays, Wednesdays and Fridays at 12:
    Music 9, History and Appreciation of the
    Clavichord
Tuesdays and Thursdays at 12:
    German 12-B
Mondays, Wednesdays and Fridays at 1:30:
    Fine Arts 6, Doric Columns, Their Uses,
    History and Heights
Tuesday and Thursday at 1:30:
    French I-C, Exceptions to the Verb Etre

"This was of course just one year's work. The next
year I followed these courses up with supplementary
courses in the History of Lace-Making, Russian Taxation
Systems Before Catherine the Great, North American
Glacial Deposits and Early Renaissance Etchers.

"This gave me a general idea of the progress of
civilization and a certain practical knowledge which has
stood me in good stead in thousands of ways since my
graduation.

"My system of studying was no less strict. In Lecture
Courses I had my notebooks arranged so that half the
page could be devoted to drawings of five pointed, exquisitely shaded stars, girls' heads, and tic-tac-toe. Some
of the drawings in my Economics notebook in the course
on Early English Trade Winds were the finest things I
have ever done. One of them was a whole tree (an oak)
with every leaf in perfect detail. Several instructors
commented on my work in this field.

"These notes I would take home after the lecture,
together with whatever supplementary reading the

course called for. Notes and textbooks would then be placed on a table under a strong lamplight. Then came the sharpening of pencils, which would perhaps take fifteen minutes. I had some of the best sharpened pencils in college. These I placed on the table beside the notes and the books.

"At this point it was necessary to light a pipe, which involved going to the table where the tobacco was. As it so happened, on the same table was a poker hand, all dealt, lying in front of a vacant chair. Four other chairs were oddly enough occupied by students, also preparing to study. It therefore resolved itself into something of a seminar, or group conference, on the courses under discussion. For example, the first student would say: 'I can't open.' The second student would perhaps say the same thing. The third student would say, 'I'll open for fifty cents.' And the seminar would be on.

"At the end of the seminar I would go back to my desk, pile the notes and books on top of each other, put the light out and go to bed, tired but happy in the realization that I had not only spent the evening busily but had helped put four of my friends through college.

"An inventory of stock acquired at college discloses the following bits of culture and erudition which have nestled in my mind after all these years.

THINGS I LEARNED FRESHMAN YEAR

1. Charlemagne either died or was born or did something with the Holy Roman Empire in 800.

2. By placing one paper bag inside another paper bag you can carry home a milkshake in it.

3. There is a double "ll" in the middle of parallel.

4. Powder rubbed on the chin will take the place of a shave if the room isn't very light.

5. French nouns ending in "aison" are feminine.

6. Almost everything you need to know about a subject is in the encyclopedia.

7. A tasty sandwich can be made by spreading peanut butter on raisin bread.

8. A floating body displaces its own weight in the liquid in which it floats.

9. A sock with a hole in the toe can be worn inside out with comparative comfort.

10. The chances are against filling an inside straight.

11. There is a law in Economics called the Law of Diminishing Returns, which means that after a certain margin is reached, returns begin to diminish. This may not be correctly stated, but there *is* a law by that name.

12. You begin tuning a mandolin with "A" and tune the other strings from that.


SOPHOMORE YEAR

1. A good imitation of measles rash can be effected by stabbing the forearm with a stiff whisk broom.

2. Queen Elizabeth was not above suspicion.

3. Nine-tenths of the girls in a girls college are not pretty.

4. The ancient Phoenicians were really Jews and got as far north as England where they operated tin mines.

5. You can get dressed much quicker in the morning if the night before when you are going to bed you take off your trousers and underdrawers at once, leaving the latter inside the former.

JUNIOR YEAR

1. Emerson left his Pastorate because he had some argument about communion.

2. All women are untrustworthy.

3. Pushing your arms back as far as they will go 50 times each day increases your chest measurement.

4. Marcus Aurelius had a son who turned out to be a bad boy.

5. Eight hours of sleep are not necessary.

6. The chances are you will never fill an inside straight.

SENIOR YEAR

1. A dinner coat looks better than full dress.

2. There is as yet no law determining what constitutes trespass in an airplane.

3. Six hours of sleep are not necessary.

4. You needn't be fully dressed if you wear a cap and gown to a nine o'clock recitation.

5. Theater tickets may be charged.

6. Flowers may be charged.

7. May is the shortest month in the year."

"The foregoing outline of my education is true enough in its way and is what people like to think about a college course. It has become quite the cynical thing to admit laughingly that college did one no good. It is part of the American credo that all the college student learns is to catch punts and dance. I had to write something like that to satisfy the editors. As a matter of fact, I learned a great deal in college and have those four years to thank for whatever I know today.

"(The above note was written to satisfy those of my instructors and financial backers who may read this. As a matter of fact, the original outline is true and I had to look up the date about Charlemagne at that.)"

Benchley's reference to "financial backers" was probably a small reference to Lillian Duryea.

It is one of the clichés of English novels that young men suffer nightmare experiences during their school years. Maugham, Huxley, Orwell and others have given accounts of what goes on in British public schools that would persuade any sensible five-year-old boy to become a dropout. Apparently New England schools were different—at least they were for Robert. His years at Exeter and Harvard were happy ones, and his notes in his diary revealed contentment with his own lot, and delight with his friends. One of his Harvard classmates was Frederick Lewis Allen who later became Editor-in-Chief of *Harper's* magazine. Another was Henry Holt, Jr., who was later to publish some of the Benchley books; Joseph P. Kennedy also happened to be in the Class of 1912.

While he was at Harvard, Robert submitted several drawings to *The Lampoon*. The first one printed was of two Irish women standing near a smelly garbage can. One of them is saying, "Ain't it offal, Mable?" He began to draw regularly for *The Lampoon*. Another classmate, Gluyas Williams, did some articles for the humor magazine, which was to be a complete reversal of roles in later life for both of them when Williams was ordained as illustrator for all the Benchley writings. All the people Robert drew looked Irish, following the cartoon custom at the time. As far back as grammar school, Robert had covered the drawings of his Latin book with pictures of Romans who looked as though their name should be O'Brien. Robert was overjoyed and rather staggered when he was elected president of *The Lampoon*—the grandeur of the office scared him. He wondered if he would be equal to it—but he needn't have worried. His performance on the job founded a Benchley tradition: both Robert Benchley's sons, Nathaniel and Robert, Jr., were presidents of *The Lampoon* in their respective years at Harvard.

Even in his college days, Benchley's gift for being *sui generis* was beginning to emerge. The combination of nobility, charm and talent—a formidable parlay—was already there. To use the word "nobility" about him as an adolescent is no exaggeration because it was already clear to anyone who met Robert that he was a person of rare inner fiber. He certainly didn't march with the drinking set, nor could he be relegated to the drones, the bookworms. He was himself, from the beginning. His after-dinner speeches at Harvard Lampoon dinners brought him all-college fame. For one, he would act the part of a headmaster talking to his "old boys" about the little school up in the hills of New Hampshire. For another, he would be a congressman telling about the legislation in Washington that lay closest to his heart. Benchley never had to start his speeches by saying "now I'm going to be the head of a school." He simply *became* a headmaster—he was an actor. By the end of his freshman year, he had been in three dramatic club plays and one Delta Upsilon play, which was an Elizabethan drama. One of his most successful after-dinner speeches was entitled, *Through the Alimentary Canal with Gun and Camera*. It dealt with Benchley's adventures in the jungle, as he pointed to imaginary lantern slides, giving direction to an imaginary lantern slide operator—and of course he had no stage properties. Nobody who ever heard these speeches could ever again listen seriously to any travelogue.

CHAPTER THREE

# "The Worst Reporter
# Even for My Age in New York"

After graduation from Harvard, the only thing Robert
could be sure of was his feeling for Gertrude Darling.
Gertrude had just left to take a position as a private
tutor in Pennsylvania, and she advised Robert not to
take a teaching job at Groton, or the Hill School, as he
had half-planned, because she felt this would keep him in
a rut. She knew even then that his possibilities were
endless. Robert spent some time in Worcester and in-
terviewed a minor official about a secretarial position at
the Boston Museum of Fine Arts. It wasn't the most
rosy prospect; the pay was $800 a year to start, a sum
which made Benchley less than ecstatic about his future
prospects, especially when he learned that the man who
was leaving the job, after six years, was making $1500.

It was one of the dullest jobs in the world, but it *was* a job, and one of the few things that kept him from going stir-crazy was knowing Mrs. Jack Gardner, the famous Boston patroness of the arts, whose protégés included Bernard Berenson. She met Robert casually, and invited him to dine at her house. The main course was fish balls, with string beans as a side dish. His second dinner at Mrs. Gardner's consisted of the same thing except that cherries rather than string beans were served. It made a strange introduction to *haut cuisine*.

At the point when the Boston Museum job was becoming even duller, the Curtis Publishing Company offered Robert a job in their New York offices as House Organ Editor. The house organ was called *Obiter Dicta*, and aside from knowing it was supposed to be a "house organ with a punch," Robert had no idea of what he really was to do. He was much more interested in getting married and was spending most of his spare time trying to convince Gertrude of this through the mails. He also spent a good deal of time at the Harvard Club and was working his way through Dr. Eliot's Five Foot Shelf. On the job, he was trying to think out his duties by writing such things as: "Conceptions of a house organ vary in picturesqueness from that of Someone's Sister, who connects it hazily with a parlor melodion, to that of the man who considers it his own literary mouth organ." When Benchley left Curtis, he said he was "given plenty of time to get my hat and coat, and they advised me to stay out of advertising, because I was too tall."

The struggles must have given Benchley permanent hard feelings about the Curtis Publishing Company, because one of the few times he ventured to be anything less than kind was when he wrote a piece about Mr. Bok's *Americanization,* an autobiography of Edward Bok. Bok had been very important at Curtis. For a long period he was editor of the highly successful *Ladies' Home Journal,* and a self-made Personality.

Benchley discusses the book as follows:

"Mr. Bok disclaims any credit for the winning ways and remarkable success of his hero, Edward Bok. Edward Bok, the little Dutch boy who landed in America in 1870 and later became the Editor of the greatest women's advertising medium in the country, is an entirely different person from the Edward Bok telling the story.

"The only connection between Edward Bok the editor and Edward Bok the autobiographer seems to be that Editor Bok allows Author Bok to have a checking account in his bank under their common name.

"Thus completely detached from his hero, Mr. Bok proceeds and is able to narrate on page three how young Edward, taunted by his Brooklyn schoolmates, gave a sound thrashing to a young bully, after which he found himself cheered by respectful boys and giggling girls who made a passageway for him to leave the schoolyard.

"He can tell how in his clear-sighted way he refused to write in the Spencerian manner prescribed in school, and he brought the Principal and the whole Board of Education to their senses.

"Mrs. Abraham Lincoln and Ralph Waldo Emerson were among the few who didn't register extreme pleasure at being approached by the smiling lad. Both Mrs. Lincoln and Emerson were failing in their minds at the time, which may explain their coolness to the author. The account of the intrusion on Emerson in Concord borders on the sacrilegious. Here was the venerable philosopher, five months before his death, when his great mind had already gone on before him, being visited by a strange lad with a passion for autographs, who sat and watched the lucid moments, making it possible for Emerson to hold his pen and form the letters of his name. (Young Edward was off with another trophy in his belt and another stride made in his progress toward Americanization. Lovers of Emerson could wish that the impersonal editor of these memoirs had omitted the account of this victory.)

"In conclusion . . . a caption under the picture of the author's grandmother: 'She counseled each of her children to make the world a better and more beautiful place to live in—a counsel which is now being carried on by her grandchildren, one of whom is Edward Bok.'

"Could detachment of author and hero ever be more complete?"

When he was not involved with house organs, or writing to Gertrude, Robert worked with the Urban League. One of his tasks was to investigate housing conditions in Harlem. He felt rather odd about bothering people in interviews, remarking about one building on East

112th Street, "They were all so clean and respectable that I felt I had no right to put them through the third degree."

He also was trying free lance writing at the time and Frank Crowninshield, the editor of *Vanity Fair*, had become interested in his work. Benchley wrote a story called, *No matter from what angle you look at it, Alice Brookhausen was a girl whom you would hesitate to invite into your own home*, and Crowninshield ran it. It was Robert's first published piece, and it made all the difference in the world to him.

Mrs. Oliver Wendell Holmes once said that Washington was full of handsome, talented men and the women they'd married when they were very young. This did not apply to the Benchley marriage. Robert Benchley was very young when in 1914 he married Gertrude Darling, his old schoolmate, in Worcester's Piedmont Church. She was the daughter of a well-to-do merchant who owned the Darling Woolen Mills in Worcester.

Gertrude was the shining exception to Mrs. Holmes' misgivings about young wives. She was good-looking, bright, and a totally independent spirit. She understood her husband and his potential from the very beginning and said—much later, "I had him so early, and I knew what his possibilities were and that I had to share him— so I did."

The Benchleys lived in a five-room apartment in Watertown for which they paid $36 a month. Robert by then had a job at the Russell Paper Company, doing personnel work. He made out lists and took care of invitations, transportation schedules, menus, etc., but it wasn't what he really wanted. When his first piece appeared in *Vanity Fair*, Robert had drawn his last ten dollars from the bank, and he was overjoyed when Crowninshield told him he had received a letter from the popular author, Rupert Hughes, saying he suspected Crowninshield himself had written the piece but "whoever this Robert C. Benchley is, let us have more of him."

To this early success, World War I came as a nightmare counterpoint. Benchley retained deep feelings about the stupidity of any war, and these were intensified by his mother's violent convictions. As a result he was rather unpopular so far as many of his friends were concerned, chauvinism being the style then. He wrote in his diary:

"Europe seems tottering on the brink of a general war . . . but I can't make it seem possible they will really fall back so far into the Middle Ages . . . If anyone is to lose I hope it is Germany and Austria on whose aggressive brutality rests the blame. Germany has declared war on England and Turkey on Servia. It is almost ludicrous in its immensity, yet frightful."

By 1915 the European war had settled down to more or less standard trench warfare. Most people considered it routine, but Robert still considered it a monstrous tragedy. There weren't enough movies made in those days to form the mass opiate they later became, but it was the time of pioneers like D. W. Griffith, and one evening Robert went to see *The Birth of a Nation*. He was appalled by something that most of the audience failed to grasp: the harm the film did to relations between blacks and whites, depicting the Ku Klux Klan as white knights slaying black dragons.

As Robert left the theater—already troubled—he heard a newsboy in the street shouting "Extra!" It was the announcement of the sinking of the *Lusitania* by a German submarine. Robert—who treasured his faith in the essential decency of mankind—found that faith to be disintegrating.

Early in October, Benchley got a very welcome letter from Franklin Pierce Adams whose Conning Tower—then in the New York *Tribune*—was the joy of civilized people at breakfast throughout the country. Adams, who had seen the *Vanity Fair* piece, wrote Benchley that he could get him on the paper as a reporter for $35 a week. One of Robert's Harvard classmates, Ernest Gruening (the first senator from Alaska, years later), was managing editor of the Boston *Traveler* then and had recommended Robert highly. He told Robert that being a reporter was almost essential training for anything Robert might do later.

The job came through at $40 a week. Robert was to be a reporter on the *Tribune*, and Adams promised him that he would soon be switched to the Sunday Section. A new supplement, the *Tribune Magazine*, was being planned, and Adams—whom Benchley respected as a leader in the dawning of civilization-in-journalism—was

to be in charge. Benchley accepted at once; he was told
to start on January 1.

Christmas that year was a meager one economically
for the Benchleys. On November 13 Gertrude had
given birth to young Nathaniel Goddard Benchley, who
was named for Robert's great-grandfather, Nathaniel
Goddard, once a deacon in Millbury, Massachusetts.
The baby was very welcome but put a crimp in the
family budget. That was the year the Benchleys sent
out a card which later became famous:

"What with the Tariff and the New Baby, we
haven't much to share this Christmas except Happiness
. . . so please don't consider it a mere Christmas formula
when we say we are hoping with all our hearts that,
between this Christmas and next, some great piece of
Good Fortune will make you fairly glow with joy, so
that, if you are superstitious, you will say, 'This is the
Benchleys Wish come true.' "

About six weeks after Nathaniel was born, Gertrude
and Bob rented the New York apartment of Gertrude's
hospital nurse, who retained her own bedroom and
kept it locked. This meant that Gertrude—new to New
York, motherhood and life among the literati—spent
her days sitting bleakly in a little dining room that had
a stark view of an outside brick wall. The apartment
was on 23rd Street and Third Avenue, just under the
El. Benchley worked from noon till midnight, so Gertrude had a great deal of time to count the bricks in
that wall. Sometimes they induced the janitor's daughter
to baby-sit while they went out to dinner. In the first

month Gertrude reckoned dinner in twenty-eight different restaurants.

As a journalist, Robert got off to a discouraging start.
He said modestly that he was "the worst reporter even
for my age in New York." This was probably because
he was too polite to ask people questions: he didn't
believe in pestering anybody. Once he was told to investigate the whipped cream machine at an expensive
French restaurant. Benchley dined there, dutifully peered
around the kitchen and found the machine coated with
"a two inch patina of curds and whey." He figured there
wasn't much he could do about it, and let the whole
thing drop.

Still, he was happy at the *Tribune*, for there were
many kindred souls on the paper: George S. Kaufman,
Heywood Broun, and others who cheered Robert's
out-of-office hours. In March, Benchley moved over to
the *Tribune Magazine*, of which Adams was editor.
There Benchley worked with Deems Taylor, and
William E. Hill, the artist.

Much later, after Benchley's death in 1945, Franklin
P. Adams wrote a letter to the New York *Herald
Tribune* describing those days.

"It is true that Benchley began his New York career
as a reporter for the *Tribune*. In the interest of added
accuracy, it may be said that it was the late Earl Derr
Biggers who wrote me that Bob Benchley ought to be
on the *Tribune*. So I went to Boston on Saturday,
November 20, 1915, and stayed that night at Mr.
Benchley's house in Watertown, Massachusetts. Mrs.

Benchley was at that time in the hospital giving birth
to Nathaniel Goddard Benchley.

"Robert Benchley came to the *Tribune* in January
1916 as a reporter, receiving $40 a week. Shortly after
that I was made editor of the Sunday graphic section of
the *Tribune*—and hired a staff consisting of Benchley,
Deems Taylor, and Irwin Edman.

"There was a lot of merriment in the Sunday department. No matter what time Benchley would arrive I
would pull out a watch and say, 'Is this what you call 9
o'clock? Go down and get your pay. You're through.'
Then Irwin Edman, a shy young man, (described by
Benchley as a 'big bully') would ask me please to give
Bob another chance.

"I can't write any more now—it makes me too sad."

The nurse's apartment depressed the Benchleys; Gertrude had become too familiar with the structure of the
brick wall. They looked around for a house and finally
chose one in Crestwood, New York, a small Westchester suburb. Robert began the life of a commuter but
it was not what he considered the ideal life. His restless-
ness was somewhat appeased by signing up in the Big
Brother movement. He became the sponsor of a German
boy from an immigrant family, and really enjoyed the
idea of helping someone in a constructive and useful way.

Frank Crowninshield, who had published Robert's
first piece, wrote to Robert at this time and asked if he
would consider substituting for P. G. Wodehouse, who
handled the Drama Page for *Vanity Fair* and was going

out to California. Robert accepted with the greatest joy. The *Vanity Fair* assignment was not a permanent one, of course, and consequently it was a blow to Benchley when Adams came to him one day and said that his job on the *Tribune Magazine* was doomed because the magazine was going to be discontinued. The employees were to receive vacation pay and that would be that. Robert tried to make a go as a free-lance writer. He did some more pieces for *Vanity Fair*, and tried the *Atlantic* and *Harper's*, as well. The pickings were slim, and when his friends told him that William A. Brady, the Broadway producer, was looking for a press agent, Robert concluded that he might be just about as good a press agent as he was a reporter. He certainly needed the job—he had made $60 in three months since he was fired from the *Tribune*.

He saw Brady in New York, and requested a salary of $75 a week. Brady made a point of reminding Robert that there were no "clocks on the job." Benchley tended to ignore clocks, in any case, and he took a great dislike to Mr. Brady. He worked at the job for about twelve weeks and hated himself, Mr. Brady, and press agentry. But every time he figured out a dramatic resignation, he remembered the $75 and the fact that Gertrude and Nathaniel were at home.

Robert wrote of his new career:

". . . I got a position as press agent which paid me twice as much as my old newspaper job, and threw me into the maelstrom of theatrical life on Broadway. Here at last it looked as if my dreams of being seduced into

some form of wickedness were coming true. You know
that theatrical crowd in New York! Hot dickety!

"If I were to list all the famous people I met in my
life in the theater you wouldn't believe me. William A.
Brady, my employer, Mrs. William A. Brady (Grace
George), Charlie the carriage starter, Julius Cohen,
an advertising man, and here was life with a vengeance
for poor little me.

"I told Mama that I was working for the Brooklyn
Rapid Transit as I didn't want her to worry. To this
day she doesn't know I was in the employ of a theatrical
producer. Neither does the theatrical producer.

"My office was on the top floor of the Playhouse in
the famous Tower Room. Here I sat all day, amid
piles and piles of old newspapers and photographs of
road companies of Mr. Brady's *Way Down East*, and
typed out stories about whichever play Miss George
was doing at the time . . .

"They didn't like to have me backstage much, but I
used to hang around the box office a bit, as there I felt
I was getting a little closer to the smell of grease paint
and the 'world of make believe.'

"Mr. Brown, manager of the Playhouse, was really
very kind hearted. One Saturday night he said to me,
smiling: 'The show closes next Saturday night. You
close tonight!'

"So that ended my Broadway career for a while and
still I had not been seduced. In all my stay among
the bright lights (2 months) I had spoken to only one
woman up in the office. She was very nice. As Miss

George was always very busy, I had met no actresses. So far New York had not got its talons into me. As I walked out of the Playhouse that cold November night— a discharged press agent—I realized that I was not only broke but, what was worse, unsullied. Neither Newspaper Row nor the Great White Way had even lifted a finger to drag me down. What was the matter with me anyway? Wasn't I pretty enough?"

Robert was rewarded for his fortitude in November of that year, when he received a telegram from his classmate, Frederick Lewis Allen, about a job in Washington with the Council for National Defense. Robert went to Washington, saw some important people and, on January 3, 1918, received a telegram confirming his appointment to the Aircraft Production Board. His job was to keep airplanes *out* of the newspapers. The family moved to a small house in Chevy Chase, next door to the Ernest Gruenings, who had also been summoned to Washington. The Gruenings and the Benchleys planted a Victory Garden together but nothing much ever came of it.

In April a Senate Investigating Committee decided the Aircraft Program was a failure and that was the end of Robert's job. In the meantime Ernest Gruening had gone back to New York as managing editor of the *Tribune* and Robert was made editor of the *Tribune Graphic*, which was an anticipation of Sunday rotogravure sections. His pay was to be $75 a week— again. Since Benchley and Gruening had always gotten along fine, Benchley looked forward to a very pleasant and rewarding job. But it didn't always work that way.

There was a little feature called the "Field of Honor" page, devoted to local boys who had been killed in action. Obviously, Robert couldn't stand the idea of sentimentalizing the horrors of war. He dealt with the matter in his own way. Gruening and he ran a picture of black troops being decorated for bravery in France; on the bottom half of the page appeared a vivid drawing of a lynching in Georgia. The top brass at the paper decided such handling of war news was pro-German, and insisted that the picture be pulled out and something else substituted.

This was at a time when anti-German feeling was at its height. Even dachshunds were considered possible spies. The owners of the *Tribune* decided Gruening—due to the stigma of his name and ancestry—was suspect. Gruening was fired without being given an opportunity to clear himself.

Benchley was horrified by this sort of behavior. He wrote a letter that went as follows:

Mr. Ogden Reid
Mr. Rogers
Mr. Garrett

Without any rational proof that Dr. Gruening was guilty of the burlesque charges made against him (except the one of living at 324 West 103rd Street) you took steps, which on the slightest examination could have been proven unwarranted, to smirch the character and newspaper career of the first man in three years

who has been able to make the *Tribune* look like a
newspaper.

I haven't the slightest idea who is boss on this sheet,
so I am handing in this resignation to the three I suspect.

(*Signed*) Robert C. Benchley

Gruening left New York and went to Alaska, where
he later made rather an impressive career for himself
as Governor and Senator.

Robert, on the other hand, began to look for another
job.

Robert was not the ideal commuter, nor was he one
to turn out a verbal pocketful of daily doings to his
wife. Living in Crestwood was quite a triumph of
conscience over matter. He kept catching cold all the
time, which may possibly have been due to the furnace.
As he put it, one of the most disagreeable phrases in
all the lexicon of disagreeable phrases is, "Well, Sam,
I guess we'll have to get the furnace fire started today.

"In his heart, the suburban house owner knows that
no objection is possible. The family had been talking
it over behind his back, and it's up to him to take care of
fuel.

"After several weeks of rigorous training (he) will
be in fair shape to face what he has to face. If it is
possible, he should stay in his retreat until it is time
to build the fire, coming home the day of the event.
He must be careful not to lose the good effect of his
rest and should refuse all invitations for the week previous. Above all, he should take no alcohol into his

system. An alternative to this prescription would be to take all the alcohol he can get just before going down cellar so that he is in a state of extreme intoxication during the procedure.

"At last the day comes; kissing his family all around and leaving his papers and insurance documents where they can be found, he descends into the cellar. It is better to have no one accompany him to witness his shame. At times like these, a man must be alone with his own soul.

"There will be no kindling ready; this is a certainty. This means that he will have to break up some boxes. It will be found that these boxes while seemingly constructed of wood are, in reality, made of a sort of marble composition which was originally put together to resist blows of axes.

"The householder apparently goes through a lot of other travail, and the next thing to do, 'is go upstairs and telephone for Jimmie, the man who makes a business of starting furnace fires in this neighborhood and keeping them going throughout the winter. This requires no more practice than knowing how to use the telephone. And is the only sure way of getting a furnace going.'"

Money, for Benchley, was simply something to spend. This trait grew stronger as time went on. Strangely enough, 1918 was, from a financial point of view, Robert's best year. Considering the large sums of money made later on, this seems at first to be a ridiculous statement. However, any bright young computer could point out that taxes and other governmental evils make all the difference. As for his personal fiscal weakness, Robert could never avoid picking up any check, of any size, on any table, anywhere, for anybody.

In this year of 1918 he made a total of five thousand and something dollars. He paid for this an income tax of $160. It was also the year the war ended, and this was a joy for Robert, who had hated every minute of it because of his own stubborn, built-in hatred of anything so uncivilized. It was another piece of good news when Frank Crowninshield asked him to come back to *Vanity Fair* for an interview.

"Would you like to be managing editor?" asked Crowninshield.

"Sure," said Robert.

It *was* a good year.

# CHAPTER FOUR

# "Ask the Sodom
# Chamber of Commerce"

*Vanity Fair* was a publication noted for its sophistication, its beautiful artwork and full-page photographs, its wit and brevity in criticism, its fine short stories and for at least three of its employees, Robert Emmet Sherwood, Robert Charles Benchley, and Dorothy Parker.

Robert Sherwood was a quiet man, about six feet seven inches tall, who had left Harvard in his junior year to join the Canadian Black Watch. At the time he joined *Vanity Fair*, he was twenty-three years old. He was listed as a drama editor and made as much as $25 a week.

Another drama editor was Mrs. Dorothy Parker. When she and Benchley and Sherwood walked down

the street together, it was said that they looked like a
moving pipe organ. Mrs. Parker was 4 ft. 11, Benchley
was about 6 feet, and Sherwood was Sherwood.

Like W. S. Gilbert's Patience, Mrs. Parker "yearned"
her living. Her poetry was self-mocking, wry and succinct; it also sold very well.

Dorothy Rothschild Parker was born in West End,
New Jersey, a mistake. She was supposed to have been
born in New York, but when she came into the world
in August 1893 she was ahead of time. She made up for
this the rest of her life, rivaling only Benchley in her
unpunctuality concerning appointments.

As Dorothy Rothschild, she was sent to a convent in
New York, and tried verse and playing the piano at
dancing school—neither of which worked out at that
particular time. When she was still very young, she got
a job writing captions for a fashion magazine. "Brevity
Is the Soul of Lingerie," was one of her inventions,
and it is still being borrowed by would-be copywriters
for today's lingerie copy.

In 1918 Dorothy Rothschild married Edwin Parker,
whose family ran a sporting goods store in Hartford,
Connecticut. Mr. Parker did not seem to get around
town as much as his bride, for no one remembers him
clearly. People tend to use words like "nice," "decent"
or "pleasant" about him. On the other hand, Mrs.
Parker, about whom the word "pleasant" was seldom
said, led a phenomenally active private life. She was
capable of platonic friendships, however, including one
that was close and enduring with Robert Benchley.

When Benchley became a drama critic, Dorothy Parker would often go along to the theater with him. At one of the first nights, a young man, who was trying to show how much he knew about the sophisticated world of the theater, ran into Benchley and Mrs. Parker. He approached Benchley and said, "And that, I suppose, would be Mrs. Benchley?"

"So I have always understood," said Mr. Benchley, "but it *is* Dorothy Parker."

The mythology on Dorothy Parker is even more extensive than that on Benchley. After all, the greatest sin against Benchley is the belief that he once said, "I must get out of these wet clothes and into a dry martini." He never said it and he didn't like it; a press agent made it up. But Mrs. Parker was credited with almost every bright, and some not so bright sayings of the 1920s.

Of course, she was responsible for a few that got around. There are the famous ones:

"*The House Beautiful* is the play lousy."

"In *The Lake*, Katharine Hepburn runs the gamut of emotions from A to B."

A telegram to the pregnant Mrs. Robert Sherwood, who had been making a great production out of the whole nine months, and had been seriously advised by Marc Connelly to "give up the whole project": GOOD WORK, MARY. WE ALL KNEW YOU HAD IT IN YOU.

When Calvin Coolidge passed away, and Mrs. Parker was told the President was dead, she replied, "How can they tell?"

When Clare Luce was defended warmly by somebody in these terms: "She's very kind to her inferiors," Mrs. Parker inquired mildly, "And where does she find them?"

In connection with some guests who were visiting Alexander Woollcott's Vermont retreat, Mrs. Parker found little to admire. In fact, one of the other guests said to her, "Where do you suppose those people go when they leave Alec's house?" To which Mrs. Parker replied, "Back into the woodwork."

Of the girls who went to a certain prom, Mrs. Parker speculated, "If they were all laid end to end, I shouldn't be at all surprised."

When she was in a hospital she gave her address as Bedpan Alley. She and Benchley were supposed to have shared an office whose cable address was Parkbench. Actually, they *thought* of doing it, but never really got around to it.

Once Dorothy Parker wrote a play with Elmer Rice, called *Close Harmony*. It didn't run very long. Mrs. Parker wired Benchley the fourth week: CLOSE HARMONY DID A COOL $90 AT THE MATINEE STOP ASK THE BOYS IN THE BACK ROOM WHAT THEY WILL HAVE.

In reviewing A. A. Milne, her famous remark, "Tonstant Weader fwowed *up*," became a classic.

When a famous actress returned from a trip to England and complained that she'd somehow picked up splinters, Mrs. Parker observed: "I suppose she got them sliding down a barrister."

Dorothy Parker was in the habit of writing suicide

notes the way other people write notes to the milkman. Her good friend Ernest Hemingway once said that "nothing in Dorothy's life became her like her almost-leaving of it." And Benchley remarked to her, after receiving the tenth or eleventh note, "Dorothy, if you keep this up, it's going to ruin your health."

In the 1930s Mrs. Parker went to Hollywood along with a great many of her friends. She wrote dialogue for a couple of movies, including one called, *The Moon Is Our Home* based on a book by Faith Baldwin, and there was actually a recognizable Parker line in it: "What's new?" said Margaret Sullavan to Henry Fonda, having been deposited in a vehicle with him suddenly and for no reason and never having seen him before.

But a couple of lines here and there did not really make for a career, or make Mrs. Parker any happier.

Her popularity and quotability got to the point where even her contribution to a game of anagrams became public material: the newspapers dutifully pointed out that she had changed the word "point" to "inkpot."

Benchley once developed a theory that everybody tended to become the person he most hated. It is not impossible to suppose that Dorothy Parker almost became the déclassé, self-pitying actress in her own story, *Glory in the Afternoon*, as well as the over-blown, suicidal heroine of *Big Blonde*, one of the saddest stories on record. It has been the curious tendency of some critics to call *Big Blonde* "corrosive." It's no such thing. It's very sentimental and gives us the other side of the Parker coin: the vulnerable, slightly

HIS LIFE AND GOOD TIMES 65

boozy lady who, under the influence of a couple of drinks, would cry at the sight of a horse being mistreated in the streets.

Where Hazel, the heroine of the story, was a stout, large-scaled woman, Mrs. Parker was of a short, loosely assembled aspect, with great spaniel eyes peering wistfully from under a thick, dark bang. She often affected picture hats and was seldom without a little dog on leash behind her.

One of her most characteristic gestures was resting her hand on her partner's while she talked, and she was made the recipient of many confidences, including one from a lady who had been married for quite a while to an extremely dull man. The lady said to Mrs. Parker, "I've kept him now for seven years!"

"Don't worry," said Mrs. Parker, pressing the lady's hand. "If you keep him long enough, he'll come back in style."

In later years Benchley was to lose patience with Mrs. Parker. He thought she was becoming too earnest, taking herself too seriously, and getting in with the wrong people. But while they were still good friends and on *Vanity Fair* together, they made it a marvelous magazine. Other contributors included: Frank Crowninshield, Arthur Symons, Gertrude Stein, P. G. Wodehouse, Amy Lowell, Hugh Walpole, G. K. Chesterton, Edna St. Vincent Millay, Noël Coward, Elinor Wylie, Deems Taylor, Carl Sandburg, Jean Cocteau, Stark Young, T. S. Eliot, Aldous Huxley, Colette, Walter de la Mare, Carl Van Vechten, George S. Kaufman, Walter

Lippmann, Heywood Broun, André Maurois, Max Beer-bohm, Arnold Bennett, Lord Dunsany, Nancy Hale, George Jean Nathan, and many others. Each issue contained handsome photographs and drawings, and two of the most popular features in *Vanity Fair* were the "We Nominate for the Hall of Fame" page and its companion-piece, "We Nominate for Oblivion."

It was ironic that a couple years after he was fired from *Vanity Fair*, Robert Benchley made "The Hall of Fame" page for the year 1924, along with Edna Ferber, Rebecca West, William Allen White, F.P.A., and Will Rogers. *Vanity Fair* said then that Benchley was "one of the most adroit and original of American humorists . . . his gift for after dinner speaking has saved many a soul blighting banquet . . . he is a discerning dramatic critic . . . he is now a diverting feature in the *Music Box Revue* . . . chiefly because he has mercifully injected into our national humor the quality of sophisticated and cultivated good taste."

Unfortunately, this was not management's view of Benchley during the years that he served with Sherwood and Mrs. Parker on the staff of the magazine. Still Mrs. Parker, Mr. Sherwood and Mr. Benchley (as they always called each other, even when they spent twenty-four hours a day together) managed to have a very good time.

Benchley also managed to do some free-lance writing. His piece called *The Social Life of the Newt* was printed in *Vanity Fair*. Benchley's style was much admired by Frank Crowninshield, but Crowninshield, unfortunately, did not make policy. The Condé Nast organization wasn't famous then for appreciation of its employees.

An office manager kept sending around memoranda forbidding employees to compare notes on salaries. Sherwood, Benchley, and Parker responded by wearing printed cards around their necks, showing their salaries in plain figures. Employees were supposed to be in at ten minutes to nine, an impossible demand on Benchley and Mrs. Parker, who were seldom on time for anything in their lives.

While the team was still together Sherwood got the idea of selling a movie script to Rex Ingram, the director, then a very important figure in Hollywood. Ingram was married to the actress, Alice Terry. Sherwood hired Delmonico's private room and invited his friends, Mary Brandon, Mrs. Parker, Mr. Benchley, Marc Connelly and a few others. This was before Sherwood's marriage—Sherwood was still courting Miss Brandon, who was later sent that famous Parker telegram.

According to Marc Connelly, a stickler for accuracy, Mary Brandon was two feet tall. Considering Mr. Sherwood's height of six feet, seven inches, he and his adored one must have made a very interesting couple.

During the evening, with the lights and the music and the drinks, gaiety became compulsory. Alice Terry kept drinking a good deal and was ill. Mrs. Parker took her to the ladies' room, brought her back, and urged more *pousse cafés* upon her. The result was that every

time Miss Terry began to feel better, her new *pousse
café* would make her feel worse, and she spent the rest
of the evening commuting with Mrs. Parker to the john.

At one point during the festivities Connelly and
Benchley went out onto the balcony. They had a little
polite argument as to who should address the peasants
in the street below. Mr. Connelly spoke first, talking to
any passersby below who would listen, promising that
Robert Benchley, as the new Prince of America, would
be very kind to the people. Mr. Benchley spoke next,
bowed, thanked the assemblage for their loyalty and
devotion, and promised many promotions and personal
gifts.

Benchley's circle of friends was in its way a rather
inbred society. Later, when Connelly married Madeline
Hurlock, Benchley and Frank Sullivan were ushers at
the wedding. Connelly claims that both Benchley and
Sullivan insisted on exercising *droit de segneur*—although that particular incident may have gained in the
translation. When Robert Sherwood and Mary Brandon
were divorced, Robert Sherwood married Madeline
Hurlock Connelly, but that's another biography . . .

Poor Crowninshield was a sort of middle man between management and his trio of obstreperous employees. It all came to a head when Mrs. Parker was fired
for a review she gave to Billie Burke.

Mrs. Parker had written, "Miss Burke is at her best
in her more serious moment; and in her desire to convey
the girlishness of the character, she plays her lighter

scenes rather as if she were giving an impersonation of Eva Tanguay," Miss Tanguay being a rather uninhibited actress of the era.

This supposedly acid slur seems pretty tame compared to what we're used to in drama criticism these days, but much umbrage was taken (more than was good for Mrs. Parker, as a matter of fact). Miss Burke objected, so did her husband, Florenz Ziegfeld, and what with one thing or another, Mrs. Parker got her pink slip very shortly. When she told her friends about it, both Benchley and Sherwood promptly wrote out their own resignations.

The newspapers were given the management's official reason for Benchley's departure: P. G. Wodehouse was returning to the magazine, which was true. But it was the end of the *Vanity Fair* idyll, if that is what it was.

One reason why it may have been idyllic was an occasional unexpected innocence on the part of the three sophisticates. To cite an example: a St. Louis housewife, a Mrs. Curran, claimed she was getting spirit messages on her Ouija board from a poetess named Patience Worth who had lived several centuries before. Crowninshield, Benchley, Mrs. Parker, and Sherwood went to visit Mrs. Curran when she was in New York and stayed to become affected by the volume of the poetry she wrote while in her trance, if not the quality. This was a sort of early day Bridey Murphy episode, and it's surprising that four such knowledgeable persons-about-town would have been as deeply impressed as they were.

On leaving *Vanity Fair*, Benchley made a resolution. He would no longer work for anybody but himself. He and Mrs. Parker rented a tiny bureau-drawer-space office on the third floor of the old Metropolitan Opera House building. It cost $30 a month, and it was here that the Parkbench cable address was discussed but never put into effect. Nor did Mrs. Parker ever write the word MEN on her door to attract more visitors. All that is in the realm of legend after the fact.

Robert's work in these magnificent quarters consisted of writing copy for an advertising agency, book reviews for the New York *World*, and other odd jobs. He also followed, as always, the dictates of his social conscience.

When the Harvard Club blackballed a man named John Macy on charges of radicalism because he had written a book about socialism, Benchley pointed out that there was very little in it to endanger the spiritual well-being of the Harvard Club members. He was upset over what he considered an unfair rejection, and sent in his own resignation. It was nonetheless vehement despite the Club's reply that he *couldn't* resign; he'd already been suspended for nonpayment of dues.

In the meantime, changes had been going on at the Benchleys' Crestwood home. Gertrude and Robert expected a new baby. There was no question; she was to be a girl, she was to be called Barbara.

When Benchley arrived at home on August 26, 1919, he found Gertrude with a baby boy. Robert, Jr., the former "Barbara" was "Robert" until Dorothy Parker caught sight of him when he was about two years old. He was a chubby baby and Mrs. Parker christened him Annie, in token of his resemblance to an Irish lady who used to work for her.

The Benchleys needed a larger home and the Crestwood house was sold. The sale of the house left some scars. As Robert put it at another time, 'You can push the forces of vengeance just so far and then down comes the ceiling! Ask the Sodom Chamber of Commerce."

He has described some of his domestic disasters: "I have always tried to be as public spirited as I could, so when it came to 'sprucing up' our home, centrally located in Westchester County, three minutes from the station, four master bedrooms and three masters, servants quarters at the foot of the plantation equipped with banjos and corn pone, I figured I could help out the situation considerably merely by fixing up the house so that the owls didn't fly in through the roof at night.

"In case your house or apartment has begun to pall on you and you are getting sick of the same old molding and the same old windows every day, just notify an agent that he may bring people around to look the place over. You'll want to stay then, just out of spite.

"People who are doing what is known as 'looking at a place' are unpleasant people in the very nature of things. They are passing judgment on a place in which you have, for better or for worse, been living for some years. There's an insult right there.

"In the first place, they always come to look when
you are in your bare feet or half your face is covered
with lather. You may have thought you kept the thing
fairly tidy, but the minute the lookers come in the
door, your house begins to look like one in a William
Faulkner novel, where poor mountain whites have
been inbreeding and cooking pork chops for generations. You can tell that these lookers wouldn't be surprised to see an old sheep stagger out of a corner. Then
they begin. You try to pay no attention and to give
them the run of the place by themselves, but you hear
them whispering or see them exchanging glances. It's
those glances that get your back up. Whatever you
may pretend to be doing while they are looking (and it
usually is something spurious, like winding your watch
or patting sofa cushions), you are burning up as they
go through the motions.

"'I suppose this is the dining room,' the woman says.
(She *supposes* it is the dining room. It's got a dining
room table and chairs and a sideboard, hasn't it? What
does she want—a steaming roast ox spread out for
her?).

"'It's not very light is it?' (It's light enough for you,
old girl. You can stand a few shadows.)

"'It might be a little more cheerful with other curtains.' (One of the reasons you want to leave may
have been the dark dining room, but right now it
seems like a sun parlor to you. Other curtains indeed.)
The lookers pass on into the kitchen where they think
they are out of earshot.

1. He would *not* sew something worsted on a card in kindergarten.

2. Robert and Edmund.

3. At Harvard.

4. Gertrude Darling
Benchley.

5. *How to Sleep* won the 1936 Academy Award for the best short subject of the year. Here we see the master taking a little hot milk before retiring, not to mention a little cold lobster, turkey, coleslaw—too bad there wasn't any milk.

6. There is a theory that if you count sheep jumping over a fence you will induce sleep. This is a fallacy, for the patient is likely to worry about one of the sheep not quite making it. (From *How to Sleep*.)

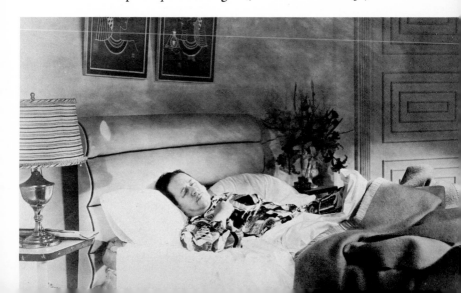

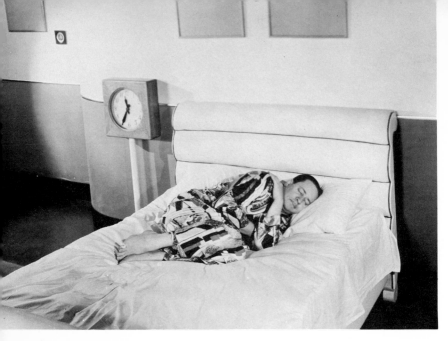

7. It is found that a sleeper changes positions fifty-five times. Let us study these positions in detail without actually getting into bed with the man. (From *How to Sleep*.)

8. The best way to get into this position is to fall into it from above. This is a great favorite with drunks. (From *How to Sleep*.)

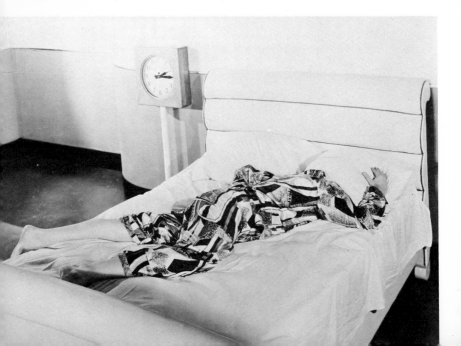

9. Back to the old refrigerator . . . he'll stay wide awake now until it's just time for the alarm to go off. Then he'll fall asleep at last. It would have been less exertion to have played a good game of handball. (From *How to Sleep*.)

10. "All aboard," yells the tongue as a cookie slips down to see The Stomach, or Prince Charming, as we shall call it from now on. (From *The Romance of Digestion*.)

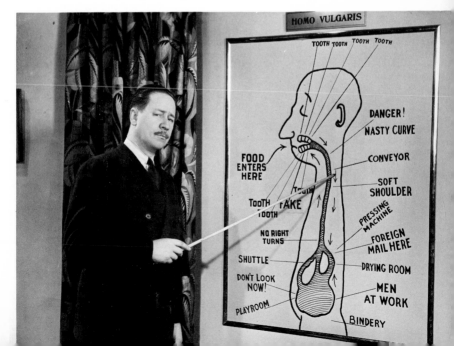

11. It is good for a boy to have a dog. A dog teaches a boy self-reliance, trustworthiness and to turn around three times before lying down. (From *How to Train a Dog*.)

12. We have a map here showing Europe and lower Antarctica, with all the trade routes. (From *No News Is Good News*.)

13. A classical criminal type, with many of the facial characteristics of Robert Benchley. (From *How to Be a Detective*.)

14. Here is where we left our bicycles. (From *Courtship of a Newt*.)

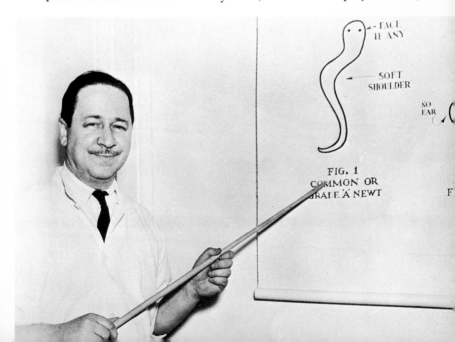

15. Does crime really pay? (From *How to Be a Detective*.)

16. A kiss from Cinderella. (From *The Romance of Digestion*.)

" 'Helma would never work here, I know.'

"Then you hear, 'Ugh.' No remark, just an Ugh. There is certainly nothing in that kitchen to go Ugh about, unless she's gotten into the ice box and doesn't like cold beets. She'd better get out of that ice box or you'll have the police on her. She's not buying cold beets from you, anyway.

"As the lookers return, surprising you at your pillow patting, you ask if they want you to show them the bedrooms. The woman smiles a nasty smile and says, 'No, they won't put you to that trouble as they have already decided (an exchange of glances) that the place is not quite large enough for them. They have a little girl. (Well, it must be a pretty big little girl to crowd them in a place this size. Pretty big, and pretty disagreeable.)

"So they leave with polite thanks which does not fool you for a minute and you come back into the dear little rooms which have never looked so good to you."

The Benchleys bought a house in Scarsdale, which Mrs. Benchley still lives in. Robert borrowed the money from Ernest Gruening, who loaned him some bonds, and from Mrs. Parker, who loaned him $200 for half an hour. (Another friend's loan reimbursed *her* at the end of the thirty minutes). Sherwood came to spend the night and the ceiling fell down, which was a sign that the new Scarsdale residents were fully qualified suburbanites.

Luckily at this time, *Life* magazine offered Benchley the job that he wanted more than anything in the
world, embodying his two loves, writing and the theater.
The job: Drama Critic.

# CHAPTER FIVE

# "The One About
# the Irishman and the Jew"

*Life* magazine in 1920 bore no relation to the magazine of the same name published today. In format it was very much like the early *New Yorker*, which in turn had borrowed freely from its British counterpart, *Punch*. *Life* printed cartoons and text on the same page, bits of verse, a full-page cartoon facing text, short pieces and articles, and full-page political cartoons. *Life* had a definite political point of view—one of its cartoons shows a troop of children going into a factory adjacent to a school; a figure labeled: "Guardian Angel" is saying, "How much better it is for them to learn something practical!"

*Life* had a lot of two-line jokes (which Harold Ross hated and wouldn't ever allow in *The New*

*Yorker*), and "Skippy," the famous urchin drawn by
Percy Crosby; it also had Dorothy Parker, Montague
Glass (inventor of Potash and Perlmutter), Marc Connelly, Arthur Kober, John Held, Jr., Oliver Herford
(his wife had a "whim of iron"), Ralph Barton and
Ring Lardner as contributors. Robert E. Sherwood
turned up as movie critic.

The advertisements were framed differently from today's. Sometimes there were several in one column;
however, nerve strain, dandruff, halitosis, perspiration
odor, and other civilized blessings were as prevalent
then as now. A book advertisement might be 5" square,
consisting mostly of a line of type announcing the
publication.

Benchley was a conscientious and excellent drama
critic. He never allowed his personal likes and dislikes
to influence his objective judgment of a play. He
wanted everybody to take Shakespeare as seriously as
he did, and of a production of *Macbeth*, he said, "It
is one of the few Shakespearean plays I can sit through."
His point was, of course, that a great deal of Shakespeare
reads better than it plays. He went on, "At this point
I sound like a young man discovering there-is-no-God."

In addition to full-length reviews, Benchley ran the
listings called "The Confidential Guide." This idea was
used by *The New Yorker*, later on, for its "Goings on
About Town" feature. All the plays in town were
described in a brief sentence to guide the theatergoer.

December 23, 1920, Benchley wrote of *Heartbreak
House* in The Confidential Guide:

"Shaw at his best in spots and wordiest in others. Altogether a delightful if over-long evening culminating in three very loud explosions."

In a later Confidential Guide Benchley wrote of *Heartbreak House*, ". . . it is for the most part very amusing and you can sleep through the scenes which aren't. (A Mr. Shaw wrote it, by the way.)"

In this December 23 issue, Benchley started his column saying, "A letter from Mr. Shaw has just arrived commenting on remarks made in these columns and an overenthusiastic audience spoiling the performance of a play by ill-timed applause. Quoting from Shaw in an offhand manner . . ."

10 Adelphi Terrace
London W.C. 2

I take in Life; and it is perhaps but natural that Life should have taken in me.

I wish that you would start a campaign against the interruption of plays by applause and laughter. Imagine an orchestral symphony stopped every three bars or so by the audience howling their delight at a pretty progression or a rousing fortissimo as operas are interrupted in Italy. I have had performances of my plays prolonged for 25 minutes beyond the rehearsal time by incontinent behavings from the very people who complain afterward that they had had to leave before the end to catch their trains. As to acting, it is impossible under such circumstances except by snatches. I have twice appealed to the London public to treat my plays as sensibly as they treat Wagner's music dramas, and not to make a noise until the curtain is down. But the musical and theatrical journalists must back me up. I am much obliged to you . . .

G.B.S.

19 November 1920

"With but slight attempt to conceal the inordinate pride felt by this department at having been designated from Number Ten Adelphi Terrace to carry on the American end of the anti-audience campaign, let it be stated that nothing could be nearer our departmental heart.

"Why should a critic spend all his time picking flaws with people on stage when fully as much harm is being done to the cause of the drama by the rabble in dinner jackets and evening gowns out front?

"They have paid their good money and are going to get it back in trade. So they loudly applaud every line that pleases them, evidently on the theory that if they make enough noise the line will be repeated for them in a few minutes. They hold up the performance when their favorite star enters . . . they think practically everything is funny . . . if they happen to like a song or dance they make it impossible for the play to go on until they have gorged themselves with six encores. And the worst of it is, they smile in a knowing manner as they do it, showing that it is deliberate. They even look about for approval . . . in fact, the theater would be much better if everyone, with the exception of me and a few of my friends, stayed at home. And even then, I should like to go alone once in a while."

Robert's legendary feud with *Abie's Irish Rose* was recorded for five long years in The Confidential Guide. He had to think up something new to say every week about this play by Anne Nichols—which he hated. His review of *Abie's* opening night had the following last paragraph: "Any further information (about the play) will be furnished at the old office of *Puck*, the comic weekly which flourished in the '90s. Although that paper is no longer in existence, there must be some old retainer still about the premises who could tell you everything that is in *Abie's Irish Rose*."

*Abie's Irish Rose* ran so long that Lorenz Hart was moved to comment, "We'll take our babies/Down to see *Abie's/Irish Rose* . . . We hope they live/to see it close."

Some of Robert's remarks about *Abie* after his initial fretfulness wore off were:

"The management sent us some pencils for Christmas so maybe it isn't so bad after all."

"We give up."

"Where do the people come from who keep this going? You don't see them out in the daytime."

"All right if you never went past the fourth grade."

"Running now for ten months—explains why Hylan is Mayor of New York."

"The world's worst and most popular comedy."

"Let's not talk about it."

"Henry Ford might be elected President—everyone scoffed when this show started."

"We refuse to answer on advice of counsel."

"The one about the Irishman and the Jew."

"A lot of people think it's funny, which makes one wonder about the soundness of a democracy."

When *Abie* finally expired in 1927, Benchley made that week's entry in a square with a black-enclosed border. All the time the feud existed, Robert was writing free-lance pieces for *Life,* most of which were collected later in his books. They ranged in subject matter from history to bedroom farce and sometimes combined both, as in his piece which begins: "It all started when the first dinosaur returned home unexpectedly . . ."

In a Paris letter dated July 13, 1922, Benchley wrote about two of his friends named Georges S. Kaufman and Marc Connellé . . . "Two young Frenchmen who have been embittered by the turn of events in France since the war—In *Camille* as well as in their earlier work, *Dulcie,* they display a cold cynicism which is so typical of the Gallic youth of today."

Once Robert said that his department would celebrate July 4th by *not* compiling a list of its favorite plays of the season. Instead, "a lawn party would be held on the grass in front of *Life*'s office, at which several actors and managers would be killed."

Soon after the *Abie* crusade Benchley relieved his hurt feelings in an imaginary talk with an Italian statesman:

Mussolini seemed to be a good man to interview; so I got an interview with him.

"Mr. Mussolini," I said, "as I understand your theory of

government, while it is not without its Greek foundations, it dates even farther back, in its essence, to the Assyrian system."

"What?" asked Mussolini.

"I said, as I understood your theory of government, while it is not without its Greek foundations, it dates even farther back to the ancient Assyrian system. Am I right?"

"Assyrian here seen Kelly? K-E-double L-Y. That was a good song, too," said Il Duce.

"A good song is right," I replied. "And now might I ask, how did you come by that beard?"

"That is not a beard," replied the Great Man. "That is my forehead. I am smooth-shaven, as a matter of fact."

"So you are, so you are," I apologized. "I was forgetting."

We both sat silent for a while, thinking of the old days in Syracuse High.

"Oh, well, then," I compromised, "have it your own way."

"I'll have it with plain water, please, and a little lemon-rind." It was the Imperator who spoke.

I signaled to the driver.

"Stop the interview," I said simply.

In a burlesque issue that *Life* put out, Benchley supplied the caption for a picture showing the Royal Coach being drawn through London streets; the view was a downward perspective. The coach was gilded and elaborate and the caption read, "Convention-Crazed Dentists Parade Through Streets of London Dragging Largest Gold Tooth in the World!"

While Benchley was on *Life* he went to see a play called *Dynamo*, taking his friend Marc Connelly with him. Naturally, Robert wore a derby to the performance and kept it on, but every time Claudette Colbert (a young actress who was making her first appearance in this play) appeared on stage, Mr. Benchley removed the derby ceremoniously. Later, during an *entr'acte* cigarette break, Benchley said, "I think it's laudable for the Theater Guild to put on a play *nobody* will like."

At home in Scarsdale Benchley was doing his bit as suburban householder and father. He alleged that most fathers in the neighborhood seemed ashamed of their noble estate: he called them . . . "a craven lot when it comes to appearing in public. They try to wheel the carriage up side streets and into empty lots, and, if they are caught leading a toddler by the hand, they try to make believe they are minding the child for some strange woman who has just disappeared. I have even seen a father hurriedly slip a cigar into his son's mouth at the approach of friends, hoping that they will think he is out with a midget business acquaintance."

Benchley faced his own fatherhood with courage in a series of pieces called "The *Life* Polar Expedition," describing how Lieutenant Commander Marc Connelly accompanied the paterfamilias from darkest Manhattan all the way to Scarsdale, putting up with untold obstacles along the way. The saga includes a section supposedly written by Robert Benchley, Jr.:

North White Plains, N.Y.—When we left Scarsdale on the second dash to the Pole my father told me that he would write the account of our trip and that I should sign my name to it, as every expedition has to have a little boy along who writes a book about it later.

"You write it and I sign it?" I asked him.

"That's right, Bobby," he said. "Daddy writes it and Bobby signs it and Bobby gets all the publicity."

"Publicity me eye," was my answer. "If I sign it, I write it. I'll take no responsibility for your drivel. I know your stuff and I prefer to write my own, *if* you don't mind. The rest of the school would kid the pants off me if one of your books came out with my name signed to it."

This angered my father and he made as if to hit me, but I ducked and ran into the house.

"All right for you, you big bully!" I yelled out at him. "Just for that I won't *go* on your old expedition."

This sobered him up and he agreed to let me write my own stuff and sign it and take ten per cent of the royalties. If the book sells as it ought to, with any kind of pushing at all from the publishers, I ought to clean up enough to marry Ruthie Henshel in the spring.

So here we are, as far as North White Plains, and very dull it has been up till now, too. We left Scarsdale at ten o'clock Wednesday morning, I on my new Demon with special coaster-brake attachment and a swell cap with a big visor on it to keep the Artic sun out of my eyes. It is my private opinion that all the Artic sun we see on this trip you could *put* in my right eye and I'd never notice it.

[*Proofreading note by Benchley, Sr.*—I *told* Bobby he ought to let me write out a rough draft for him first. You see what he has done with "Arctic." However, if he is going to be just stubborn about the thing—]

The trouble with the expedition so far is that my father and Lieutenant Commander Connelly get winded so soon. They can't pump up even a little hill without having to get off at the top and rest. We're lucky to be at North White Plains, let alone the North Pole. I began by going on ahead as fast as I could, but this just made them sore and I lost them going through Hartsdale and had to sit down by the roadside and wait for them to come up. They both got pretty fat during the summer hanging around at the base in Scarsdale, and my father especially has got to look out or he'll look something awful in another year. I told him so, too, and he told me to shut up or he'd send me away to military school.

Well, anyway, what with the old folks puffing along behind and Ensign Thermaline having to stop off in White Plains to see an old girl of his, it has taken us just four days to get this far.

Coming through White Plains, my father tried to tell me about the battle that was fought there during the Revolutionary War.

"What battle was that?" I asked.

"The Battle of White Plains, of course," he said. "What did you think it was, the Battle of Princeton, N.J.?"

"Princeton beat Harvard, didn't they?" I came back at him.

At this he made a lunge for me, and fell off his bicycle, which got me to laughing so hard I had to stop, too.

"And who won the Battle of White Plains, Father dear?" I asked him, trying to change the subject.

"The Americans did, of course," he said, brushing himself off.

"Yeah?" I said. "So the Americans won, did they? Well, that shows what *you* know about it. The British won. We had it in school only last week."

"What school?" asked my father, very sore now.

"Not Harvard, anyway," I said. "Yale beat Harvard, too."

"Yeah?" he said, getting redder and redder. "Yale beat Harvard by playing twelve men against Harvard's eleven . . . And if you aren't a better boy, Daddy's going to send you right back to Scarsdale on the 4:10 from White Plains."

"The 4:10 doesn't stop at Scarsdale," I said. "It's an express to 125th St."

"Let's be getting on," interrupted Lieutenant Commander Connelly. "This is no way to get to the North Pole—arguing about Harvard and Yale."

So we all got on our wheels again and pushed ahead, but I think I'll drop off at Mt. Kisco and see the Barry kids. My time is worth *something*.


In real life, our North Pole correspondent, little Bobby Benchley, was having a confrontation with his father on the issue of nailbiting. This habit was passed down *directly* from the father's side of the family to young Robert.

When Benchley was home one weekend, Gertrude said, "You'll have to speak to the child about his fingernails." Robert, Sr. dutifully took his younger son into another room.

"O.K., let's see the nails" . . . this was delivered in a loud voice. Then, in a very low voice, "See if you can bite them down as far as I do."

Naturally, Robert, Jr. giggled. Robert, Sr. replied, "Quiet. Be sure you go out whining!"

As it happened, Robert, Jr. didn't bite his nails for two months. Maybe Benchley was more of a child psychologist than he ever wanted to be. He may have avoided children in the abstract, but he had their number:

"In America," he wrote, "there are two classes of travel—First Class, and With Children.

"Traveling with children corresponds roughly to traveling third class in Bulgaria. They tell me there is nothing lower in the world than third class Bulgarian travel.

"There are several branches of the ordeal of going on Choo-Choo, and it is difficult to tell which is the roughest. Those who have taken a very small baby on a train maintain that this ranks as pleasure along with having a nerve killed. On the other hand, those whose wee companions are in the romping stage, simply laugh at the claims of the first group.

". . . the final phase of the ordeal however is in store for you when you make your way into the diner . . . it turns out that the nearest thing they have suited to your child's customary diet is veal cutlets. Everything else has peppers or sardines in it. A curry of lamb across the way strikes the boy's fancy and he demands that. On being told that he hasn't the slightest chance in the world of getting it, he becomes quite upset and threatens to throw a fork at the Episcopal clergyman sitting opposite. Pieces of toast are waved alluringly in front of him and he is asked to consider the advantages of preserved figs and cream, but it's curry of lamb or he gets off the train. He doesn't act like this at home—in fact, he is noted for his tractability. There seems to be something about the train that brings out all the worst that is in him: all the hidden traits he has inherited from his mother's side of the family. There is nothing to do but say firmly, 'Very well then, son. We'll go back without any nice dinner,' and carry him protesting from the diner.

"In fact, I had a cousin who had to take three of his little ones on an all-day trip from Philadelphia to Boston. It was the hottest day of the year and my cousin had on a woolen suit. By the time he reached Hartford, people in the car noticed he had only two children with him. At Worcester he had only one. No one knew what had become of the others and no one asked. It seemed better not to. He reached Boston alone and never explained what had become of the tiny tots."

# CHAPTER SIX

# "So, on the Way to the Theater"

"They weren't what they were cracked up to be," said James Thurber, a few years ago. "That bunch at the Algonquin insulted each other all the time. If you said to one of them, 'How are you,' he'd answer, 'Better than you are, old boy!'"

This was one man's opinion, and it must be added that James Thurber was excluding Robert Benchley from this damnation. He had referred to Benchley earlier as "the president of chivalry." Thurber simply didn't enjoy the insult-humor that seemed to characterize the Round Table in its later years.

The Round Table's headquarters, the Algonquin Hotel, came into being when Frank Case, a determined, bright young man, shuffled out of Buffalo to find his

fortune in New York. He managed to wangle owner-
ship of a building near the corner of Sixth Avenue and
44th Street. At the public library he looked up a pleas-
ant-sounding Indian name that was friendly and cheerful. As a tribe the Algonquins weren't particularly pleasant or friendly or even cheerful, but as the name of a
hotel, Algonquin came off brilliantly.

It was from the beginning a *nice* hotel, and many
well-heeled old families came there for the Case hos-
pitality. But the proprietor cared more about writers,
musicians, and artists. Streams (or maybe at first riv-
ulets) of actors began to trickle in. Raymond Hitchcock, a matinee idol of the day, threw a huge party
there and among his guests could be discerned the fore-
runners of the Round Table: the Fred Stones, Rex
Beach, Sam Harris, Douglas Fairbanks, Ethel Barrymore, Flo Ziegfeld . . .

When the Round Table as we know it today began,
when the twentieth century reached its own twenties,
its members didn't yet amount to very much. They
were still in a wistful, peering-at-the-future stage. Case
had an instinct for quality, though, and, what was more
important then, he allowed credit and charged low
prices.

The Round Table's King Arthur was F.P.A. To be
printed in his Conning Tower column in the *Tribune*
(and later on in the *World*) was the acid test of literary
acclaim: if you wrote well, briefly and meaningfully,
Adams would use your piece. An admirer of Adams,
George S. Kaufman, began to drop in at the Algonquin,

and so did his collaborator, Marc Connelly; there followed Deems Taylor, Edna Ferber, Neysa McMein,
Heywood Broun, Alec Woollcott, Robert Benchley
. . . the table became a legend in no time at all.
Ambitious squares (pseudo-intellectuals, gossip colum-
nists and other bores) were turned away. Some of them
have survived and claim to be remnants of the Round
Table, but if all the claimants had ever actually been
seated the dining room would never have held them.

Young Robert Benchley, Jr., the notorious nailbiter,
lunched and dined with his parents at the Algonquin
so often that he was convinced it was the only place
to eat in New York. Once, for no particular reason,
Gertrude took Bob, Jr., to the Astor for lunch. The
child stared at the hangings and decorations in the
Hunting Room and remarked: "They've changed the
Algonquin, haven't they?"

Nobody ever said, "Let's be selective and start a
Round Table"; it just happened. Alexander Woollcott
was one of its chief touters. In those days, Woollcott
ran the world of Literary Criticism like a Mafia chief-
tain. If he admired a book so did fifty thousand club-
women; it was *Mr. Chips* or else. Luckily, aside from a
few odd whimsies, Woollcott's taste was catholic and
sensible. His first anthology contained Anthony Hope's
*The Dolly Dialogues*, a splendid unappreciated novel
*Kamongo* by Homer Smith, and the debut of Evelyn
Waugh in America with *A Handful of Dust*, possibly
at Benchley's suggestion, all of which Woollcott him-

self called (understatement was not his downfall) "adventures in the realms of gold."

At the lunch table in 1928 the Algonquin featured Lobster Newburg at $1.25, Roast Lamb at $1.50, Filet Mignon at $1.25, and most desserts at under 50¢. At the time the Round Table started, some eight years or so before, the prices were about half that amount. It cost marvelously little to be in peerless company and to have Frank Case listen sympathetically to hard-luck stories or listen happily to intimations of success.

By the end of the 1920s the Algonquin had turned into a sightseer's paradise, especially the dining room. It was, after all, the time of a special flowering of civilization—humorists bursting into first-rate importance. There was certainly no such thing then as a soi-disant "literary establishment" (the phrase would have been jeered at) with its roots in a few blocks of Manhattan. On the contrary, the sayings of Mrs. Parker, Mr. Benchley, Mr. Woollcott, and assorted friends were on a magic national tom-tom service. There was an unwritten law about would-be joiners of the Round Table: nobody was allowed who dealt in pedantry, and each member started with a high quotient of quick-thinking and considerable personal charm.

It has become the custom to lump all humorists, with the possible exception of Aristophanes, Congreve and Mark Twain, as "Algonquin wits." But while the membership *was* elastic, the circle didn't even include

some of the great humorists of the era, such as Ring
Lardner. Some years ago, a writer doing a book on
Lardner asked Mrs. Parker what she remembered about
him. She replied, "I never knew him very well. I don't
think any of us did." And that is close to truth. Benchley
was a great admirer of Lardner. Once, at a Dutch Treat
production of one of the brief nonsense plays which
Lardner did so brilliantly, Benchley caught sight of
Lardner's wife, Ellis. Benchley didn't know who she
was, but began talking to her and praised the play
highly. Ellis said, "Oh, I think it's terrible." Benchley
looked at her with horror and walked away. Later on
he found out who she was and came sliding back across
the floor, ending up on his knees calling, "Forgive me!
I didn't know!"

In 1927 Ring Lardner wrote a play called *Dinner
Bridge* (it ran for fifteen minutes and scorned plot or
consecutive action) for another Dutch Treat occasion.
Edmund Wilson published it that year in the *New
Republic;* when it was presented, the cast was rather
unusual: Robert Benchley, George S. Kaufman, Percy
Hammond, and Robert Sherwood.

The luncheon group at the Algonquin was an informal one—and it was highly critical of other people's
work. The members decided to put on a review of their
own. They had no idea what the show would be about,
so they bought all the tickets themselves and passed
them out to friends.

This was Robert's chance to resume his career, begun at Harvard, as an actor. Here is his account of what was certainly the turning-point of his life:

"Some years ago, I was made a member of a committee to plan a little Sunday night entertainment for some newspaper men who wanted to act. The committee was supposed to meet at a certain time, each member with suggestions for sketches of song numbers. (I will come right out and say that the 'certain time' at which the committee was to meet was 8 P.M. on a Sunday night.) At 7:15 P.M. I suddenly realized that I had no suggestion to offer for the entertainment. As all other members of the committee were conscientious workers, I felt considerably abashed. But as they were also charming and indulgent people, I knew they would take my dereliction in good part if I could only take their minds off the business of the meeting and possibly put them in good humor with a comical story or card trick. So, on the way to the theater, I decided to make believe, when they called on me for my contribution, that I had misunderstood the purpose of the committee meeting and had come prepared to account for last year's expenditures. These I jotted down on the back of an old shirt.

"As is always the case with such elaborate trickery, my plan to censure by diverting the minds of the committee fell flat. They listened to my temporizing report and voted me a droll chap, but then they said: 'And now what are your suggestions for the entertainment?' As I had to confess that I had none, it was agreed that I should elaborate the report I had just offered and perhaps acquire some skill in its delivery, and give that as my share of the Sunday night entertainment.

"At this moment, my entire life changed its course."

*"The report is delivered by an Assistant Treasurer who has been called in to pinch-hit for the regular Treasurer who is ill. He is not a very good public-speaker, this assistant, but after a few minutes of confusion is caught up by the spell of his own oratory and is hard to stop.*

"I shall take but a very few moments of your time this evening, for I realize that you would much rather be listening to this interesting entertainment than to a dry financial statement . . . but I *am* reminded of a story—which you have probably all of you heard.

"It seems that there were these two Irishmen walking down the street when they came to a—oh, I should have said in the first place that the parrot which was hanging out in *front* of the store—or rather belonging to one of these two fellows—the *first* Irishman, that is—was—well, *any*way, this parrot—

*"(After a slight cogitation, he realizes that, for all practical purposes, the story is as good as lost; so he abandons it entirely and, stepping forward, drops his facile, story-telling manner and assumes a quite spurious businesslike air.)*

"Now, in connection with reading this report, there are one or two points which Dr. Murnie wanted brought up in connection with it, and he has asked me to bring them up in connec—to bring them up.

"In the first place, there is the question of the work which we are trying to do up there at our little place at Silver Lake, a work which we feel not only fills a very definite need in the community but also fills a very definite need—er—in the community. I don't think that many members of the Society realize just how big the work is that we are trying to do up there. For instance, I don't think that it is generally known that most of our boys are between the age of fourteen. We feel that, by taking the boy at this age, we can get closer to his real nature—for a boy *has* a very real nature, you may be sure—and bring him into closer touch not only with the school, the parents, and with each other, but also with the town in which they live, the country to whose flag they pay allegiance, and to the—ah—(*trailing off*) town in which they live.

"Now the fourth point which Dr. Murnie wanted brought up was that in connection with the installation of the new furnace last Fall. There seems to have been considerable talk going around about this not having been done quite as economically as it might—have—been—done, when, as a matter of fact, the whole thing *was* done just as economically as possible—in fact, even *more* so. I have here a report of the Furnace Committee, showing just how the whole thing was handled from start to finish.

"(*Reads from report, with considerable initial difficulty with the stiff covers.*)

"Bids were submitted by the following firms of furnace contractors, with a clause stating that if we did not engage a firm to do the work for us we should pay them nothing for submitting the bids. This clause alone saved us a great deal of money.

"The following firms then, submitted bids:

"Merkle, Wybigant Co., the Eureka Dust Bin and Shaker Co., The Elite Furnace Shop, and Harris, Birnbauer and Harris. The bid of Merkle, Wybigant being the lowest, Harris Birnbauer were selected to do the job.

"(*Here a page is evidently missing from the report, and a hurried search is carried on through all the pages, without result.*)

"Well, that pretty well clears up that end of the work.

"Those of you who contributed so generously last year to the floating hospital have probably wondered what became of the money. I was speaking on this subject only last week at our up-town branch, and, after the meeting, a dear little lady, dressed all in lavender, came up on the platform, and, laying her hand on my arm, said: 'Mr. So-and-So (calling me by name), Mr. So-and-So, what the hell did you do with all the money we gave you last year?' Well, I just laughed and pushed her off the platform, but it has occurred to the committee that perhaps some of you, like that little old lady, would be interested in knowing the disposition of the funds.

"Now, Mr. Rossiter, unfortunately our treasurer— or rather Mr. Rossiter our *treasurer, unfortunately* is confined at his home tonight with a bad head-cold and

I have been asked (*he hears someone whispering at him from the wings, but decides to ignore it*) and I have been asked if I would (*the whisperer will not be denied, so he goes over to the entrance and receives a brief message, returning beaming and laughing to himself*). Well, the joke seems to be on me! Mr. Rossiter has *pneumonia!*

"Following then, is a summary of the Treasurer's Report:

"(*Reads, in a very businesslike manner.*)

"During the year 1929—and by that is meant 1928—the Choral Society received the following in donations:

| | |
|---|---:|
| B. L. G. ................................. | $500 |
| G. K. M. ................................. | 500 |
| Lottie and Nellie W. ——————  .......... | 500 |
| In memory of a happy summer at Rye Beach .. | 10 |
| Proceeds of a sale of coats and hats left in the boat-house ............................ | 14.55 |
| And then the Junior League gave a performance of "Pinafore" for the benefit of the Fund, which, unfortunately, resulted in a deficit of ....... | 300 |
| Then, from dues and charges ................ | 2,354.75 |
| And, following the installation of the new furnace, a saving in coal amounting to $374.75—which made Dr. Murnie very happy, you may be sure. | |
| Making a total of receipts amounting to ..... | 3,645.75 |

"This is all, of course, reckoned as of June.

"In the matter of expenditures, the Club has not been so fortunate. There was the unsettled condition of business, and the late Spring, to contend with, resulting in the following—er—rather discouraging figures, I am afraid.

| | |
|---|---:|
| Expenditures .......................... | $23,574.85 |
| Then there was a loss, owing to—several things—of .......................... | 3,326.70 |
| Car-fare .............................. | 4,452.25 |
| And then, Mrs. Rawlins' expense account, when she went down to see the work they are doing in Baltimore, came to $256.50, but I am sure that you will all agree that it was worth it to find out—er—what they are doing in Baltimore. | |
| And then, under the general head of Odds and Ends .............................. | 2,537.50 |
| Making a total disbursement of (*hurriedly*) | $416,546.75 |

Or a net deficit of—ah—several thousand dollars.

"Now, these figures bring us down only to October. In October my sister was married, and the house was all torn up, and in the general confusion we lost track of the figures for May and August. All those wishing the *approximate* figures for May and August, however, may obtain them from me in the vestry after the dinner, where I will be with pledge cards for those of you who wish to subscribe over and above your annual dues, and I hope that each and every one of you here tonight will look deep into his heart and (*archly*) into his pocketbook, and see if he cannot find it there to help us to put this thing over with a bang (*accompanied by a wholly ineffectual gesture representing a bang*)

and to help and make this just the biggest and best
year the Armenians have ever had . . . I thank you.

"(*Exits, bumping into proscenium.*)"

The show called *No, Sirree!* opened the night of Sunday, April 30, 1922, at the 49th Street Theater. The
*Treasurer's Report* was something new and mysteriously attractive. Among those giggling helplessly in the
audience were Irving Berlin and his partner, Sam H.
Harris. They offered Robert a spot in their *Music Box
Revue* delivering the *Treasurer's Report*.

Robert Benchley felt strongly that as a drama critic
he didn't have any business parading around the stage
as an actor. Still he never knew how to say no. He
told Harris and Berlin that he wanted $500 a week,
which seemed to him an outrageous sum, one that
they would certainly refuse. Harris said, "O.K., but
you'd better be good."

As Robert himself says, "I guess no one ever got
so sick of anything as I, and all my friends, have
grown of this *Treasurer's Report*. I did it every night
and two matinees a week for nine months in the third
*Music Box Revue*. Following that, I did it for ten weeks
in vaudeville around the country. I did it at banquets,
at teas, at friends' houses, in my own house, and finally
went to Hollywood and made a talking movie of it.
In fact, I have inflicted it on the public in every con-
ceivable way except over the radio. And dropping it
from airplanes." (But he was wrong. Later he did

deliver it over the radio, and to studio audiences before his radio show began.)

Apparently Benchley was the only one who felt this way about the *Treasurer's Report*. Everybody else loved it.

The scintillating talk at the Round Table wasn't the result of two martinis at lunch; coffee, tea and orange juice were the liquid stimulants. This was the era of Prohibition, the Noble Experiment, and the Benchleys were militant Drys. Robert's New England upbringing had instilled him with a dislike for liquor; in any case, he objected to breaking a law. He also found it difficult to understand why people would spend so much money for something that made them sound so *foolish*.

There are various legends about how Robert was fed his first drink. One has it that Donald Ogden Stewart gave it to him at the Yale Club late one afternoon. Another story is that Frank Crowninshield gave a dinner once for Benchley, Don Stewart, Deems Taylor, and others. Everybody was drinking but Benchley, who refused politely.

Stewart said, "What's the matter—are you a Holy Roller?"

So Robert took a drink, a manhattan.

In any case, the first drink led to a great many others. Benchley's drinking capacity was one of the marvels of the age. With all his intake—which was later to start about five in the afternoon and go on for ten or more hours—very few people saw him drunk. The only time Benchley was ever reckoned to be in a state of intoxication was one night at the Stork Club, in the '30s, during a drinking contest. According to the ground rules devised by the contestants, each had to order and down what his opponent was drinking when the contest began. A crowd collected to watch and cheer: Bob's opponent soon disappeared under the table. Benchley sighed with relief and said, "May I order something I like now—a scotch and soda?" He was escorted back to his room that night by a policeman who found him walking up and down outside the Club. Benchley then bought the policeman and himself a drink.

It became increasingly clear that Robert couldn't continue with the schedule of a commuter. Appearing every night in the *Music Box Revue* and having to cover first nights besides was just too hard on him.

Benchley lived briefly with Donald Ogden Stewart in an apartment furnished with little besides a rowing machine. For reasons best known to himself, Benchley used it while wearing white gloves. Later he and Charles MacArthur shared an apartment on Madison Avenue.

This was some time before the famous night when Romeo and Juliet were replaced temporarily as legendary lovers: MacArthur had met Helen Hayes at a party, handed her a bowl of peanuts, and said, "I wish they were emeralds." (But after the MacArthur-Hayes nuptials the new Mrs. MacArthur considered Benchley a bad influence on Charlie. From then on, they didn't

see each other a great deal, although there was no loss
of affection.)

During the Benchley-MacArthur domestic arrangement, MacArthur decided to invite Paul Robeson, the
baritone, to lunch at a well-known club. Benchley said
he'd love to come, too, with Gertrude. In those days
it was simply not done to take blacks to lunch. Particularly, it was not the function of black waiters at a
first-rate club to serve black entertainers. The party of
MacArthur, Mr. and Mrs. Benchley and Robeson was
seated behind a small, hastily constructed screen, where
they would not offend the sensibilities of the busboys
and waiters who found it demeaning to serve Mr. Robeson. The tempers of the guests did not improve as the
lunch wore on.

At home Gertrude hired a Jamaican maid named
Rosa, who delighted MacArthur on the weekends
Benchley brought him along. "How's your immortal
soul?" Charlie would yell, and Rosa would reply,
"*Mine's* fine, Mr. MacArthur, how's *yours?*" And they
would outdo each other in Bible-quoting.

In one of the darkest moments in the history of
finance, Benchley, Dorothy Parker and Donald Ogden
Stewart opened a joint bank account. Benchley's experiences with banks were never entirely happy. At
one point the president of the Scarsdale Bank had to
put a thousand dollars in Robert's account when it was
overdrawn; Gertrude told Robert to thank him. Robert
said, "Why should I? He forged my name, didn't he?"

This same bank president asked Robert for tickets

to the *Music Box Revue* for a friend. When the banker found out that Robert had had to pay for the tickets, he insisted on making good. Robert had the money changed into pennies, and brought the loot to the bank in a paper sack. The bag broke on the Scarsdale bank floor.

As Benchley says, "There are several bank accounts of mine which the *bank* forgot, but none that I can recall offhand where I was the dreamy party. I have sometimes forgotten that I didn't have a bank account, and have drawn checks on which not even the *date* was valid, but try as I will, I cannot think of any bank to which I can go and say: 'Oh, by the way, what ever became of that old balance I had here some years ago?'

"The decent thing for any bank to do, if it finds itself with some old account of mine that I have overlooked, is to get in touch with me. I'm home practically all day every day and the telephone is right by my bed. It would be my pleasure to put on some clothes and go down to the bank myself to see about it if they would only let me know. I might not even wait to put on some clothes.

"I have never used passbooks in my banking, as the cashier usually says: 'Never mind actually depositing this, Mr. Benchley. I'll just keep it in my pocket until you need it.' Later on I began carrying it in my *own* pocket until I needed it. As a result, I have no actual written evidence that I have any money in any bank at all."

While Robert was in the *Music Box Revue*, he stopped
in one day at the Hotel Biltmore and was enchanted by
the girl who was in charge of Western Union there.
Her name was Carol Goodner. She had light brown
hair; she was pretty and charming, and Benchley decided she should have a part in the show. So she began
a theatrical career, with a great deal of help from the
drama critic of *Life*. It was a career of some note—she
became a popular, sought-after leading lady not only
in New York but in England. She appeared on Broadway in *The Man Who Came to Dinner* and *The First
Mrs. Fraser*, among many other hits.

Carol Goodner and Robert were seen often around
New York together. They were a familiar sight at
Tony's, ("The *Original* Tony's") and at the restaurant
that was the forerunner of "21," in those days at 42
West 49th Street. One of Benchley's books, *The Early
Worm*, mentioned in its acknowledgments the fact that
Garol Goodner had suggested the title. Carol Goodner
remained Benchley's companion until just about the
time of the opening of *The Garrick Gaieties* which was,
in 1925, a departure in the musical theater.

Benchley referred to it as "The most civilized show
in town." It was put on by the Theater Guild and the
program note read, "*The Garrick Gaieties* believes not
only in abolishing the star system, it believes in abolishing the stars. The members of *The Garrick Gaieties*
were recruited, impressed, mobilized or drafted from
the ranks of *Caesar and Cleopatra*, *The Guardsman*,

*St. Joan, They Knew What They Wanted,* and other Theater Guild productions."

Some of the members of *The Garrick Gaieties* were Alvah C. Bessie, Romney Brent, Harold Clurman, June Cochrane, Lorenz Hart, Elsbeth Holman (she later changed that Elsbeth to Libby), Sterling Holloway, House Jameson, Philip Loeb, Edith Meiser, Sanford Meisner, Richard Rodgers, and Lee Strasberg.

There was also a gifted young comedienne who could dance and sing and interest Benchley. Her name was Betty Starbuck.

She was born in Brooklyn. By the time she was fifteen she found out she was able to entertain people at parties; naturally, she wanted to go on the stage. One of Betty Starbuck's colleagues in *The Garrick Gaieties* in recalling those days, said that Betty had had a very sad childhood because of an alcoholic father and innumerable domestic brawls.

Benchley was fascinated by Miss Starbuck. She was tall and extremely willowy with big blue eyes and close-cropped brown hair. Both Richard Rodgers and Herbert Fields were very much interested in her and tried to use her in all their shows—but Benchley took up too much of her time that should have been spent at rehearsals.

Benchley was a good critic off the job as well as on of Betty's acting ability. For a play called *Wild Waves* with Osgood Perkins, Benchley objected to Betty smoking a cigarette on stage: "For God's sake, don't smoke. It isn't like you." They cut out the cigarette business from the scene. And for several years, Benchley had a great deal to say about the public and personal life of his protégée.

# CHAPTER SEVEN

# "Robert Benchley, His Corner . . ."

"I feel sorry for anyone who wasn't twenty in the '20s," remarked one of Miss Starbuck's theatrical colleagues, recently. "Betty and I had such marvelous times! It was a breakthrough in manners and morals. For the first time theater people were being accepted in circles they hadn't moved in before; parties were given for them by the Big Names in Society. *The Garrick Gaieties* cast was making the-then-Equity-minimum of $35 a week. Naturally, we couldn't tip the servants at the elegant estates we visited. We used to leave on the milk train Sunday mornings to get out of leaving something for the maids.

"Once all the girls in the show wore striped men's-bathing suits and appeared ensemble on a Long Island beach, claiming we were the Widows and Orphans of

Celibate Seamen. Boys from Princeton, Yale and Harvard would follow us around, and take us dancing at the Lorraine Grill, the Plaza, and to Harlem late at night. We wore those chiffon frocks with uneven hems, silk stockings with clocks, satin pumps with Baby Louis heels and cloche hats . . .

"You know who the best dancer was? You'll never guess. It was William Beebe, the bathysphere man; he was just a wonderful dancer."

Betty Starbuck appeared in two editions of *The Garrick Gaieties*, in *Peggy Ann* in 1926, *Chee-Chee*, *Heads Up*, *Hello Daddy*, and a couple of other plays long forgotten by audiences.

Much later on, when Benchley was the drama critic of *The New Yorker* magazine his note on a theater program for a show he and Miss Starbuck attended read, "Betty is the best listener and co-laugher . . . and she's a wasted comic."

Betty Starbuck's ancestors were Nantucket people, and she used to love to practice New England dialect. Her favorite menu was one that included "bahtlett payuhs and sugar squayuhs. Ayeh."

One evening Betty had a date with Robert at "21." She arrived on time, sat down at a table and waited. And waited. A few hours later she received a message: Robert had gone to see some friends off for Europe. The ship was to sail at midnight. While a jolly party was going on in a cabin on "A" Deck, Robert was so carried away that he was *literally* carried away.

Betty Starbuck became very much a part of Benchley's set of friends. She and Dorothy Parker would
trade insults. Betty found Mrs. Parker witty and barbed
and "not very pleasant." But an actress who knew them
well at that time claims Betty tried to imitate Mrs.
Parker in speech. She would make little wicked comments about her friends in a style that was really not
like her at all. On the other hand, when anyone tried
to say anything unkind directly to Betty, she would turn
vulnerable and defenseless.

The Benchley-Starbuck romance went on for quite
a while. Back in 1921 the Benchleys had bought a house
in Siasconset and Robert spent many summers there.
Most of his friends were guests, including Betty Starbuck, who was very fond of Mrs. Benchley.

When Robert Benchley, Jr. was nine years old he
was taken to a Betty Starbuck opening. On the way
to the theater he banged his thumb in a taxi door.
It was too late to do anything about it at the time,
but backstage, between the acts, Robert, Jr. got to
sit on Betty's lap. He says that it was just about that
*moment*, actually, that he became aware of the opposite
sex. Nathaniel Benchley, then in his early teens, apparently had a wild crush of his own on Betty Starbuck.

Neither Betty Starbuck, nor anyone else among the
ladies who adored him, really influenced Benchley's
feeling about his family. It was clear always that his
family came first.

Donald Ogden Stewart said, much later, that the

Benchley marriage was one of the strongest he ever knew. And it was during the twenties that Bob made out his Will. It was a very simple Will, which read: "Confident that she will adequately provide for our two sons and any child hereafter born to us, I make no provision for them, but give all my property to my wife, Gertrude Darling Benchley, absolutely, appointing her Executrix without security.

"Witness my hand and seal the 23rd day of February, signed Robert C. Benchley."

In the 1930s Betty Starbuck married Edward W. Burr, Jr. whom she had known all her life. He was a broker. They settled in Riverside, Connecticut, and Betty took a job in a book store. She credited her interest in books to Robert. Pygmalion Benchley had been at it again— Betty had been turned into a fanatical reader.

Recently there was a 25th anniversary celebration of *The Garrick Gaieties*. Among the missing were Lee Strasberg, who may have been busy at the Actor's Studio, and Alvah Bessie, who used to be a chorus boy but became a writer. Among those who turned up were Sterling Holloway (now a collector of avant garde art), Libby Holman, Edith Meiser, Romney Brent—and Betty Starbuck.

In 1921 Robert Benchley's first book of collected pieces appeared, published by his classmate, Henry Holt. It was called *Of All Things*. Holt was one of a group of people who used to hang around Jack & Charlie's, which was then at 42 West 49th Street. After the bar closed at 1 A.M., the regular crowd would remain: Holt, Monte Brice, Frank Morgan, Ernest Boyd and Benchley, each with his own bottle, sitting at a table and talking about life. After Jack & Charlie's closed, they would travel up to Harlem, to such places as Dickie Wells', the Nest, or the Savoy Ballroom. Once Brice was given a Mickey Finn after making the rounds with Benchley, who saw that Brice got home, unconscious but safe.

Jack Kriendler and Charlie Berns were the original founders and partners of "21." At first they had two clubs in the Village. Later they opened the 49th Street place. Subsequently, other members of the family became active in the clubs: four Kriendler brothers, H. Peter, called Pete, Maxwell A., called Mac, I. Robert, called Bob, and Jack, who was John Carl Kriendler. There were two Bernses, Charlie and H. Jerome.

Mac Kriendler, in talking about Benchley, says, "He taught me to drink." (This was quite a switch for a relative of a speakeasy owner.) "I was in law school then. One day when I felt tired, Bob said, 'Have a drink.' It was a Suisette—Pernod, white of egg, and a touch of sugar. It made me less tired."

Often Mac would go to Harlem with Benchley and his friends. One night in midtown New York they hit thirty-eight speakeasies, all on the same block; 52nd Street. Robert had his usual supply, Mac had a beer or two—his conversion was a slow one.

One night at "21" Benchley, to amuse his friends, tried a magician's act that involved a carnation. He tried to make it disappear but he couldn't. Not wanting to let anyone down, he ate the flower—and was sick to his stomach.

Mac Kriendler says, "He taught me the language; he told me it was important to read a portion of the dictionary every day."

Another favorite hangout for Bob and his friends in the '20s was "The Original Tony's," where other regulars were Dwight Deere Wiman ("The gentleman producer"), Heywood Broun and F.P.A.

Tony Soma, a small, athletic, amiable man who still runs a restaurant called "Tony's Wife" in New York, was a waiter at the Knickerbocker Hotel and then at the McAlpin, during Prohibition. He knew a dentist who could get "scotch" that Tony later sold for $10 a bottle; the dentist got it from a longshoreman. That's how Tony became a speakeasy operator who started to sell liquor just about the same time Benchley started to drink it. Tony put it this way: "The public needed a man who was used to smuggling. I was doing a service to humanity, to the intelligentsia."

In 1929, six months before the Kriendlers moved their restaurant, Tony moved to 59 West 52nd Street. He kept the liquor at 57 West, in the house in which he and his family lived. One night when Tony was talking to Franchot Tone's mother, (a suffragette and devotee of supper clubs; she and Franchot would never appear in the same ones), Broun brought in some people who had been with him at "21." At that moment some agents yelled "Raid!" Benchley wrote four figures on a piece of paper which he slipped to Tony. Luckily Tony did not need the money Benchley indicated he was willing to lend. The place was closed for only one day.

Tony took great pride in the fact that so many of his clientele were "intelligentsia." He also took great care of the actresses, particularly the ones he thought of as ladies. He would never allow Edith Meiser or Betty Starbuck to have more than two drinks. He would just smile and stop listening to their orders. Tony's customers were his friends and often confided in him. Benchley told him one night about an evening he and Dorothy Parker, and Carol Goodner spent as guests of bankers at an elegant home after a perfomance of *Charlot's Revue*. They drank and talked and then they all stole souvenirs to take home. When Tony liked a customer, he would perform for him by standing on his head and singing opera, a custom in which he still indulges for favored clientele.

When the site of the original Tony's was given over to Rockefeller Plaza, and construction had begun, Benchley said, "Hey, I want my swagger stick. I left it at Tony's."

Tony's was the only speakeasy never to have a checkroom girl. It was a family place, no strangers were allowed, and the Somas knew personally every guest or friends-of-guests. The first Mrs. Soma was very stern about manners, and once told Lucius Beebe, "If you don't take your hat off, you don't get any martinis." Mr. Beebe removed his top hat.

Charlie Berns, who is still active at "21," tells how Mike Romanoff in those days was always looking for a handout, and always got one from Benchley. Later, Benchley used Romanoff's Restaurant in Hollywood as his West Coast "21," and claimed that Romanoff was the only man who could use the phrase "enlisted men" and make it sound like "illicit men."

As Berns recalls, "Bob would go to Tony's, as well as our place—but our food was better. Then, after a lot of the clubs were raided they analyzed all the liquor. Ours was found best. Bob was pleased; it vindicated him in a way, and the general public was beginning to catch on. But he was, in a large measure, responsible for our early success."

Success is an understatement for what has happened to "21." It is probably the most celebrated restaurant in the world, and Mac Kriendler and Charlie Berns are on intimate terms with almost every luminary in the Western—or for that matter, Eastern—world.

Today at "21," there is a metal plaque, put in shortly after the death of Robert Benchley. It is over the table where he always sat, not far from the kitchen, and it reads: *Robert Benchley, His Corner, 1889–1945.*

In his rounds of speakeasies, Benchley would collect stories about two of his favorite people. They happened to be Prohibition agents: Izzy Einstein and Moe Smith. Izzy was a bulbous little man who decided to become a law enforcement agent when he read that they made up to $2500 a year. He was told he didn't look like a detective, and this was very true. Izzy was forty years old, bald, just over five feet tall and weighed over 200 lbs., most of which was in the middle. It made him look like a Santa Claus toy (knock-it-down, it-springs-right-back) weighted in the middle.

One of Izzy's first jobs was to clean up a Brooklyn speakeasy, which was suspected of breaking the law because drunks had been seen staggering from the place and, for blocks around, the air was enough to make a teetotaler stagger. Nobody had ever been able to get inside the building until Izzy Einstein—who knew nothing about conventional police procedures—walked up and knocked on the door. A peephole was opened and somebody said, "Who's there?"

"Izzy Einstein," said Izzy. "I want a drink."

The voice demanded to know who sent him and what his business was.

"I'm a Prohibition agent," said Izzy. "I just got made one."

The doorman slapped Izzy on the shoulders. "That's a good one," he said. "That's the best gag we've heard in this place yet." Naturally, Izzy was shown off to the guests and to the bartender, but when he was given a drink he found he couldn't make the arrest. He had drunk the evidence.

From that time on he kept a small funnel in the upper pocket of his vest and connected it with a rubber tube to a bottle concealed in the lining of his garment. Now, whenever Izzy got a drink, the funnel took over after a while. This stunt gained him many, many arrests.

Izzy's partner, Moe Smith, was also a natural comic. He was an inch or two taller than Izzy and wasn't quite so round. He didn't have the natural-comedian look, but he was good foil for Izzy. The New York *Tribune* called Izzy the "mastermind of the federal rum ferrets."

Benchley, a solid admirer of the pair, enjoyed their ingenuity. It delighted him when Izzy and Moe came one evening to a speakeasy where many false tries had been made for an arrest. The bartender simply wouldn't give drinks to anybody he didn't know. Izzy and Moe went out of the place again—it was the coldest winter night in history. Izzy stood in front of the speakeasy in his shirtsleeves until his teeth chattered. Moe carried him inside again shouting: "Give this man a drink! He's just been bitten by a frost!" The bartender was startled by this emergency and rushed forward with whiskey. Moe snatched the bottle and arrested him.

One of their customs was to play "How Dry I Am" on the trombone, if the speakeasy was apt to be frequented by musicians. When they went to posh places they would appear with two pretty girls and wear dinner jackets, with brilliantine in their hair and jeweled studs in their shirt fronts—their way of blending into the scenery.

During their career together in the bootleg era, Izzy and Moe confiscated some five million bottles of booze, smashed an enormous quantity of speakeasy fixtures, and made almost five thousand arrests. No other agents ever approached this record.

By 1925, there had been so many stories about Izzy and Moe in the newspapers that the Prohibition enforcement officials in Washington became quite miffed: they never got *their* names in the papers. Izzy was called to Washington and told to conduct himself as a "subordinate, not the whole show."

By this time Izzy and Moe were public figures and if reporters couldn't get real stories about them they made them up. The boys were sadly missed when they turned in their badges. For some people, including Benchley and his friends, they were the noblest chapter in the Noble Experiment.

In addition to Tony's and "21," Benchley and company enjoyed the Club Durant, which was run by Jimmy Durante and his partners, Lou Clayton and Eddie Jackson. There was also the Sutton Club where Beatrice Lillie sang, while Fred and Adele Astaire danced at the Trocadero. Then there was Helen Morgan singing at Dutch Schultz's Embassy Club. These places represented the higher brackets of speakeasy life in New York. Benchley and his companions were familiar faces at every one of them.

Benchley recognized the perils of his deep distrust of daylight hours. As he said, "No matter where I am, if there are more than four people assembled in party formation, I must always be the last to leave. I may not be having a very good time; in fact, I may wish that I had never come at all. But I can't seem to bring myself to say, 'Well, I guess I'll be toddling along.'

"Other people are able to guess they'll be toddling along. One by one and two by two, and sometimes in great groups, I watch them toddle along until I am left with possibly just my host to keep me company. Sometimes even my host asks me if I mind if *he* toddles along to bed. When this happens, I am pretty quick to take the hint. I have often thought of hiring a little man to go about with me just to say to my host: 'Well, Old Bob thinks he will be toddling along now.' It's that initial plunge that I can't seem to negotiate. It isn't that I can't toddle. It's that I can't *guess* I'll toddle."

The best after-hours club for Benchley was a rather famous institution run by Miss Polly Adler. Polly's was used by a variety of people for a variety of reasons, but Benchley liked it because it was never closed. He could never go to bed—it was as simple as that. He had to stay up later than anyone else.

Polly moved around a lot. She was first on Madison Avenue, then on the west side of New York, Riverside Drive and other locations, according to the whim of the police.

Unlike most of Polly's clientele, Benchley would ask for an empty room saying he wanted a good night's sleep because he had a magazine piece due. Sometimes, if he had a deadline to meet, he'd stay on at Polly's until he finished. No matter how casual his schedule seemed, his pieces were always done with the greatest care, were given the most exquisite polish, and the copy always looked as if a professional typist had turned it out.

Benchley often said that his best articles were written at Polly's, or as he pronounced it, Pawly's. One naïve young lady always thought Benchley was talking about visiting a suburban family when he said, "Let's all go up to Pawly's"—something he said quite frequently.

There was a Negro maid employed by Miss Adler who adored Benchley and performed valet services for him. When Bob would arrive and retreat to his empty room, the maid would immediately get to work pressing his suit and laundering his shirt, socks, and underwear. She even shaved Bob in the mornings, and he claimed that her smile at breakfast lit up his life.

With breakfast at around eleven-thirty, on a typical day, Benchley might fool around with the typewriter for a while (either at Polly's or his hotel), and then saunter out for a late lunch at the Algonquin with the rest of the Vicious Circle. The afternoon might be the time to answer mail, to telephone Gertrude in Scarsdale, or to drop in on old friends visiting from the coast—Douglas Fairbanks, Roland Young or other movie cronies. At six or seven Benchley would call in at Tony's or "21" for drinks, then off to the theater to cover a first night for *Life*—then back to "21" for dinner, and on to Harlem and perhaps another after-hours club. A long day and a merry one. He spent a good deal of time in taxicabs and used to puzzle many drivers by urging on them a device he had invented to help remember which New York streets went which way: "Evens East, Odds Bodkins."

# CHAPTER EIGHT

# "Everybody Had Fun but the Lady Who Dusted"

Benchley was not only the ideal companion, he was basically a person of true, instinctive courtesy. One of his close friends, Howard Dietz, said that he was "the most entertaining personality ever to deck the tables of New York and Hollywood." Dietz added that it was quite possible that Benchley was at times unhappy but, if so, nobody ever knew it. "Benchley would have considered it discourteous to let anyone think he wasn't having a good time."

This courtesy was never forced. Half the wonder of being with Benchley lay in the fact that Benchley wasn't only funny, he laughed out loud at everybody else's jokes. Anyone who was with him became convinced that he and Benchley were the two funniest people

17. The courtly trio disbanded when Mary Pickford sent Doug Fairbanks a wire COME HOME AT ONCE.

18. Reading about the death of Little Nell.

19. As to humor, I can only tell you what Schwanzleben said in his work, *Humor After Death*. He hits on this point indirectly when he writes, "All laughter is a muscular rigidity spasmodically relieved by involuntary twitching."

20. According to Dr. Le Noix, an eminent French scientist who happened to be sleeping across the foot of my bed....(From *Courtship of the Newt*.)

21. Some of the drawings in my economics notebook were the finest things I have ever done.

22. I sometimes go into a corner and cry.

23. You may even become a mystery man.

24. A strong offensive is the best defense.

5. I always have had trou-
le in adding and subtract-
ng 7's and 8's.

26. One day I look like Wimpy.

alive. Most people feel there's a lot more to them than
the world ever sees—Benchley was the man to bring it
all out. Other writers admired him in a way unusual for
writers. Thurber said that certain Benchley pieces predated his own Walter Mitty. Thurber and Benchley
often got around to writing the same sort of piece and
worrying vaguely that it had already been done by the
other.

The year 1926 was an important one for Benchley,
partly because it was the first time he became part of a
Hollywood scene. He'd been asked to work on some
scripts at the Fox lot, and this coincided with a wedding
invitation from his old friend, Don Stewart, who was
marrying Beatrice Ames. At the bachelor party the
night before the wedding, Benchley went outside
Stewart's Malibu beach house to find a bathroom. He
walked onto a dock, hit a flight of steps "going in the
wrong direction," and threw his knee out. He refused
to let this interfere with his part in the wedding and
performed his duties as best man with his leg in a cast.
Later he was told he might have to have an operation on
the knee, but he never bothered about it.

Benchley charmed everyone at the Fox studios, and
Tom Chalmers, one of the executive heads, decided
Benchley should act in movies as well as write them.
That was how the famous Benchley shorts began to ap-
pear. First (of course), *The Treasurer's Report* and,
second, *The Sex Life of the Polyp*.

Of these first appearances, Benchley said: "I do not
intend ever to take part in a motion picture again until

I am a well-known star, so that people will actually recognize me on the street when they see me. This halfway recognition is driving me crazy. Last summer I played a small part in a small picture. The role was not impressive enough to affix itself or me in the minds of audiences as a definite motion picture character. All they know, when they pass me on the street, is that they have seen that face before, under not very attractive circumstances."

Of course, later on, That Face did become a rather famous one. He described it once himself: "One day I look like Wimpy, the hamburger fancier in Popeye, another day it may be Wallace Beery. Some mornings if I look in the mirror soon enough after getting out of bed, there is no resemblance to any character at all, either in or out of fiction, and I turn quickly to look behind me convinced that a stranger has spent the night with me and is peering over my shoulder in a sinister fashion merely to frighten me. On such occasion, the shock of finding that I am actually the possessor of the face in the mirror is sufficient to send me scurrying back to bed completely unnerved.

"I have never seen a meaner face than mine in hat store mirrors. I could stand its not being handsome, I could even stand looking weak in an attractive, man-about-town sort of way. But the mirror confronts me with a hang-dog face, the face of a yellow craven, while even though I may have had a haircut that very day, there is an unkempt fringe showing over my collar and back and the collar itself seems to be something

which would be worn by a Maine guide when he goes
into Portland for the day." Benchley referred another
time to this problem: "Somehow, when I got all dressed
up, I looked like a house detective."

He claimed that this furtively familiar look led to all
sorts of interviews, like one instigated by a reporter who
asked Benchley for a list of the ten most people in the
world.

"The *ten* most?" I asked.

"Ten or eleven most," replied the reporter.

"I could name you the ten least people in the world,"
I said, "but the ten most—well, first I would nominate
Ahmed Bey."

I had him there because there was no such person as
Ahmed Bey.

"Okay," he said, "now we're getting somewhere. See
what we can get done when you stop fooling?"

His Hollywood visits were short ones during the
1920s, and his life was based in the East. He had been
living in New York at the Hotel Algonquin, where he
knew everybody, everybody loved him, and the Round
Table was right downstairs. But that was the trouble.
He kept *going* downstairs and couldn't get his work
done. So he moved across the street to the Hotel Royalton, where there weren't any public rooms downstairs
and he thought he would be able to get a great deal
accomplished.

Benchley had an idea that the furniture in his rooms
at the Royalton looked Victorian. His admiration for
this look started him on a new career as receiver of

rejected or stolen ugly furniture: ". . . a long time ago I set out to furnish a room in a sort of knickknack fashion. I even invited contributions from my friends, but what I meant was contributions that I could use. I didn't mean I was starting a whaling museum or that I planned to build more rooms on. I had more or less in mind a mid-Victorian study of the 'what not' variety. Well, I got my 'what-nots.'

"It began with little articles to line up on top of a bookcase, miniature geese, little men with baskets, shells with eggs in them and broken stags. Everyone had fun but the lady who dusted.

"Then people began looking around town for heavier gifts. It got to be a game. Trucks began arriving with old busts of Sir Walter Scott, four-foot statues of men whose shirt fronts lit up when attached to an electric connection, stuffed owls and fox terriers that had lain too long at the taxidermist's. This phase ended with the gift of a small two-headed calf in a moderate state of preservation. From then on the slogan became 'Send it to Benchley.' Chipped cornices from the old post office, detached flights of stairs, hitching posts and railings began pouring in. Every day was like Christmas in Pompeii. The overflow went into the bedroom and I started sleeping under an old spinet covered over with a set of bead curtains which had been brought back to me from a bordello in Marseilles.

"The friendly mood in which the game started changed gradually to one of persecution. Once the Missing Persons Bureau took a hand in it and searched my rooms for a runaway college girl. They found nothing however, but three Chinese laborers, who had been smuggled into the country and delivered to my place in a caterer's wagon."

One entered Robert's room through a little vestibule, which was filled with magazines, canes, swords, telephone messages and bric-a-brac. The living room itself was red, and a green student-lamp gave an atmosphere of a small, ill-run New England college. There was a couch which Bob used to call the track, because when he wanted to take a nap he'd say, "I guess I'll do a couple of laps around the track," and then he'd go to sleep on it. Robert Benchley, Jr. said that lying on it gave a person a strange look like a wirephoto; your face would be streaked in horizontal lines.

Robert's books were all around the room, and very odd ones they were. (*Success with Small Fruits, Bicycling for Ladies* and *Keeping a Single Cow.*) There was also a model of an Erie steamboat, a cello and music stand, Brueghel prints, some beer mugs, and framed pictures from the old *Life* magazine.

There was a closet between the bookcases containing a banjo, a Fire Chief's hat from Worcester, peanut butter, suitcases, and jars of New England boiled dressing. Benchley did his writing on a small table, which was very hard to find.

The bedroom was just big enough for a single bed, a dresser and one person.

Among the absurd books in the living room was his

collection of material concerning the Queen Anne period which he admired and wanted to write a book about. He longed to do this all his life. After he died, Gertrude Benchley turned over his Queen Anne collection to the library at Exeter. Benchley had ambitions as well to write at least two novels. One was to be about a man, a big shot in Prohibition days, who lived on the recognition awarded him by speakeasy owners—what would he do when Repeal came, where was his fame? The other was to be about people who knew they had first-rate potential but would never get to the top.

Benchley actually had started work on his study of the Queen Anne period, but when he got the typewriter going and looked at the paper in the roller it said, "I was looking through my desk the other night and I came across a lot of old snow . . ." That became a different kind of piece, and the serious one about Queen Anne never did get written.

One of the many visitors to Benchley's rooms and one of his best friends was John Hay Whitney. Don Stewart had introduced them. Whitney recalls in a masterpiece of understatement, "We were both around the town then." Benchley and Whitney took to each other from the first. Robert wrote in a letter to Jennie in Worcester: "Jock Whitney is the finest young man I have ever met."

Whitney remembers the rooms at the Royalton mostly for the clutter, those beaded curtains—which separated the bedroom from the living room—the books that were piled all over, the red cloth-covered table, and the student lamp. When the room at the Royalton was taken apart after Benchley's death, it was Whitney who showed up to call for the beaded curtains. Looking very dignified and ambassadorial, he murmured that the curtains "had been in the family for years," although it was general knowledge that Don Stewart had stolen them from the Marseilles bordello.

Whitney and Benchley went to a lot of first nights together. Whitney recalls that Benchley was an extremely earnest critic. He resented humorous asides by companions and wouldn't pay any attention to his friends while he was taking notes. They both had a serious interest in the theater. Occasionally Whitney would invest, and when he and Benchley were given the script of *Life with Father* they agreed that it would never go. "You see, I was right," said Benchley to Whitney, during opening night intermission, still thinking it was pretty tame stuff.

One year, Whitney, Benchley, and Whitney's future brother-in-law, James Altemus, chartered one of the first private planes to tour Europe. They traveled through all the capitals by night because they had to do the flying by day.

Benchley describes that trip as follows:

"It seems very funny that, with all this talk of transoceanic fliers, nothing has ever got around about the big Benchley endurance flight from London to Budapest in March of this current year.

"I can't really say that the idea of flying to Budapest from London was mine. I had had some notion of going by train. In fact, I had the trains all looked up and marked in red on the timetable. But not one of them was ever used, except once when I missed the plane. During our preliminary stay in London I lived in the fool's paradise of thinking we were going to Budapest like other people.

"The two young men who were fortunate enough to be my traveling companions at the moment (and whom I will call Luther and Erman just in kidding) had, it seems, other plans. By the way, Luther and Erman have been pretty well identified from their police records as John Hay Whitney and James D. Altemus. They didn't say anything about the plans to me at the time because they wanted the whole thing to come as a surprise and partly because I'm older than they are and have soberer judgment in such matters as flying to Budapest. As a matter of fact, granting me a wee bit of precocity in adolescence and a certain laxity in state marriage laws, I am old enough to be their father but really more of a pal than a father. . . ."

(Whitney usually referred to Benchley as "Gramps," a habit which Benchley's own family took up, as well as a lot of other people.)

"So, on the morning of March 6th when we left our hotel in London for Paris, I was under the impression that we were headed for the most charming of trains, the *Golden Arrow*. I was very gay at the thought of the Channel crossing, for I am a good sailor and had reason to believe that Luther was not. 'Never mind, Luther,' I said, 'Gramps will tell you all about the big ships we pass if you can't see them yourself.' It was not until we had been driving for half an hour that I sensed trouble. This was followed by considerable giggling on the part of the boys. Just then we turned sharply to the right next to a big sign which said CROYDON.

"'What are we going to do, *fly* to Paris?' I said, joining in the laughter. 'I didn't bring my helmet.' I can joke as well as the next man.

"'We've got a helmet for you, Gramps,' said Luther. 'And a dandy little parachute, too, in case you want to get up and pick some daisies along the way.'

"I looked at Whitney, er, I mean Luther, suspiciously between narrowed eyelids but as I had been out late the night before they couldn't tell the difference between that look and the one I'd had all morning. And even as I withered them with my glance we turned in at the big airdrome at Croydon and piled out like a crowd of happy school boys. 'Well lads,' I said, 'Gramps will be going back to London now. And the best of luck to you!'

"But I said it rather weakly for I knew I was caught. I had never flown before and had often boasted that I never would fly, not so long as my ankles held out. But I really couldn't see any way out of this box unless I were to fall down and play dead. And even then the boys would probably have taken me in the plane to Paris for burial, so that was out. My only course was to spoil their little joke by making believe I didn't care.

"'You young scoundrels,' I said, laughing, 'how did you know I wanted to fly to Paris? Ha, ha, ha, I haven't flown since the war.'

"'What war was that, Gramps?' asked Erman, 'the War of the Roses?'

"Luther and Erman were looking at the map and talking with a pilot in flying togs when I rushed up to join them. 'Toughest kind of luck, boys,' I said. 'No more passenger planes out today. Fog over the Channel.'

"'O.K. here!' said Luther. 'That means we'll have less traffic to get through. Anyway,' added Luther, 'you can't go to London without your umbrella.' This was a poser. 'You boys aren't going to fly this private plane yourselves, are you,' I asked. 'Just a little now and then,' said Erman. 'I've got a pilot's license, you know.' 'So had Mark Twain,' I said, 'but a Mississippi River steamer has different controls from an airplane.' 'Oh, they all work on the same principle,' said Erman, 'don't they, Luther?' 'Sure,' said Luther, 'all you have to do is not look down and Gramps, if you are a good boy maybe you can fly a little, too. Won't that be fun?'

"There, on the concrete plaza, stood the *City of Melbourne*, with her twin motors roaring as pretty as anything you would care to see somebody else going up in. I started to run over in my mind all the sins of my past life but had only gotten as far as my sixteenth year when somebody said, 'Up you go, Gramps,' and sure enough up I went.

"It is now my plan to tell some of the more technical details of the flight, and, although this expedition was unique in that it was not made in the interests of aviation, perhaps some of the facts recorded here may be of value to fliers who plan to go over the same route in the future."

(Whitney revealed much later that there was no heat in the plane, and they all had to run up and down to keep warm.)

"In the first place, keep your eyes shut. This does away with what is known as 'flier's disease, or throw-up,' and if you happen to be a little sleepy when you get into the plane, it may result in a refreshing doze. I myself shut my eyes as we left the ground at Croydon and before I knew it was lulled by the drone of the motors into a fitful but life-giving sleep. When I awoke we were swooping down onto the field at Le Bourget.

"Emerging from the cabin after a perfect landing, I approached the first official in sight and said modestly, 'I am Charles Lindbergh.'

"There was a tremendous crowd on hand to see us land, the word having gotten around Paris that we were on our way, but most of them were busy wheeling our baggage into the waiting room and the other two didn't seem to care. So after nibbling at the sandwich they keep in the restaurant there for emergencies (Lindbergh is said to have taken the first bite out of it, although the ham has been changed since), we soon found ourselves in Paris, ready for a good night's sleep (100 francs extra with wine)."

Luther, or Whitney, as we may now call him, claims that once in a railroad carriage in Germany Benchley saw a woman wrestling with a stuck window. He was very proud of his language skill, and was also very

chivalrous. He went over to her and said in flawless
German, "May I help you?" She looked at him, paused;
then she belted him.

One of the most important events of the 1930 social
season was John Hay Whitney's marriage to Liz Altemus. Adele Astaire was bridesmaid, Fred Astaire was an
usher, and Robert Benchley was the best man.

Gertrude Benchley decided not to go to the Whitney
wedding. "I kept myself too much in the background,"
she admitted much later; but her feeling was unshakeable
about her husband being permitted to lead a life of his
own.

The night before the Altemus-Whitney wedding in
Philadelphia, there was a large party given for the
groom. There was a great deal of celebration and Bob
was drinking enough to feel the need of fresh air. He
walked out of the house, and kept walking, up and
down unfamiliar streets in the dark, pleasant air, and
was finally drawn to a big brilliantly lighted house
where the sounds of music and laughter caused him to do
something he'd never in his life done before. Benchley
said to himself, "I want to go to that party," and he
walked right up to the door and went in and crashed
the party—which turned out to be the same one he had
started from.

Benchley's fondness for John Hay Whitney extended
to Whitney's mother. In a copy of *The Treasurer's
Report*, Benchley wrote, "For Helen Whitney, in recognition of her services in bringing the *Aquitania* safe into

port after one of the roughest and what seemed to be also one of the shortest voyages across the Atlantic—or *was* it the Atlantic? Bob Benchley."

Benchley once said that one of the pleasantest little ironies of life was to be with Jock Whitney around a piano, a frequent occurrence in those days at parties given for theatrical people, listening to Whitney sing:

> *"Gee, but it's tough to be broke, dear,*
> *It's not a joke, dear, it's a curse. . . ."*

# CHAPTER NINE

# "I Find That I Get Too Sore About It . . ."

Summers were a pleasant change of pace from the Royalton-Algonquin-21-Harlem rounds. Benchley spent as many vacations as his jobs would permit at Siasconset, on the island of Nantucket, with his family. The New England strain in him responded completely to the sea, the sand and even the fog. The house was a rambling wooden structure with a porch, and it was in the midst of a beginning-colony of writers and actors. One of the neighbors was Patricia Collinge, well known as an actress then but more famous later for her role as Birdie in Lillian Hellman's *The Little Foxes*. Miss Collinge had always respected Benchley highly as a critic because he never made an actor suffer. Still, because he was a critic, she was in awe of him, despite his modesty

and shyness. She soon got to know him better in the
relaxed Siasconset social life. She remembers him at
parties, pleasant, affable and charming but quick to
leave the room quietly if somebody offended his notion
of good taste. At one gathering, for example, one of the
men did an act involving some puppets with hand-
motions that were rather crude. Benchley didn't say
anything; he just walked into another room and read a
book.

Like many others who spent a good deal of time
with Benchley, Patricia Collinge was struck by his sense
of fairness. "He *hated* injustice of any kind," she told
an interviewer. "Whenever he saw it, he tried to put it
right."

This was a time that was sorely in need of such a
sensitive conscience. For most of the 1920s, the decent
people of the world had been appalled by an apparent
miscarriage of justice—a court action that is still con-
troversial and unsettled: the Sacco-Vanzetti case, in
which Benchley played an unexpected role.

In 1921 Robert and Gertrude Benchley had gone
back to Worcester to see Jennie and to spend a weekend
with some old friends. Saturday, Robert drove over to
the country club to pick up his host. Later that night,
at dinner, Benchley learned that his friend had been
talking to Judge Webster Thayer in the clubhouse. At
the time Thayer was presiding in the Sacco-Vanzetti
case, and Thayer had told Benchley's friend privately:
"A bunch of parlor radicals are trying to get those

Italian bastards off. I'll see them hanged and I'd like to hang a few dozen of the radicals, too."

On July 14, 1921, Sacco and Vanzetti were found guilty of shooting and killing a paymaster and his guard during a payroll robbery in Braintree, Massachusetts. There began an agonizing period of appeals and motions. Public interest in the case increased with every new development. Proper Boston ladies became champions of the underdogs, church groups demanded inquiries; people all over the world became involved with the case, both emotionally and financially. Felix Frankfurter, then a professor at Harvard Law School, wrote an article in the *Atlantic Monthly* in which he charged prejudice on the part of the jury, the prosecution, the witnesses, the community, and particularly the judge.

H. G. Wells, Romain Rolland, John Galsworthy, Isadora Duncan, Thomas Mann, Albert Einstein, and Anatole France were among those who wrote strongly against the conviction of these men. Vanzetti is supposed to have said ". . . our words—our lives—our pains—nothing! The taking of our lives—lives of a good shoemaker and a poor fish peddler—all! That last moment belonged to us—that agony is our triumph!"

(Years later James Thurber and Elliott Nugent were able to stir audiences in the theater when they used this moving speech as an important part of their play *The Male Animal*, produced first in 1940 and revived during the Joseph McCarthy era, when the speech was even more pertinent.)

On May 4, 1927, Vanzetti sent an appeal for a new

trial to Governor Alvan T. Fuller of Massachusetts.
The appeal was accompanied by five affidavits, one of
them Robert Benchley's. Robert made a legal deposition
giving his account of what had happened at his friend's
home the night that he and Gertrude had dined there
and he had heard about Judge Thayer's quoted remarks.

However, at that point Benchley's friend denied the
whole thing. He (the friend) had grown up with
Thayer—perhaps his memory was influenced by that.
Benchley's affidavit was not admissible in court because
it was hearsay evidence, but it was printed in the
*Boston Evening Transcript* of May 5, 1927.

Governor Fuller in the meantime appointed a committee, consisting of Abbott Lawrence Lowell, Samuel
Wesley Stratton, and Robert Grant, to study the trial
and make a report to him. Fuller had been elected in
1924, defeating the famous James M. Curley for the
Governorship of Massachusetts by the largest majority
in the history of the state.

Benchley went up to Boston and repeated his testimony before the committee. Then he went to Governor
Fuller and once more told his story. Fuller didn't seem
to put much stock in it. He mentioned that he himself
often told stories and embroidered them a bit to make
them more pointed. He asked Robert if that wasn't
perhaps what he was doing in recounting what Thayer
was supposed to have said. Robert was given some
pages of testimony and was asked to go through them
indicating places where prejudice appeared. When Rob-

ert returned to New York and studied the testimony, he wrote to Fuller:

". . . please bear in mind that the judge who is being quoted is the same man who *one week before* told his golfmates in the locker room of the Worcester Golf Club that he would 'get these Reds good and proper.'"

He concluded, "I'm afraid this has been a pretty long letter. I hope it has not been so long but that you have been able to read some of it. I have no personal interest in this case and in fact have tried not to think about it any more than I could help, because I find that I get too sore about it if I do. But Massachusetts in my home state. . . . I feel very strongly—just as you do—that it is concerned here."

The committee's decision was that Sacco and Vanzetti were guilty. On August 3 Governor Fuller announced he would not spare them.

At this point Judge Thayer was called in to rule on a motion for a new trial based on a charge of prejudice on the part of the trial judge. To nobody's surprise he turned this down.

Governor Fuller did grant another respite, this time until August 22. On August 10 petitions for a writ of habeas corpus were rejected by Justice Oliver Wendell Holmes and a Circuit Court Judge, George W. Anderson. On August 23, 1927, Sacco and Vanzetti were executed.

There is no doubt that Benchley had tried valiantly to do what he considered the just thing. And there is also no doubt that many of his friends were brought into the matter through his interest in it: Dorothy Parker immediately went up to Boston to parade in a demonstration for the good shoemaker and the poor fish peddler. When she got back to New York Robert said to her, "Did they take your fingerprints?"

Mrs. Parker looked at her bare arms ruefully and answered, "No, but I have a lot of theirs."

Katherine Anne Porter, Harry Emerson Fosdick, John Dewey, Arthur Schlesinger, Sr., H. L. Mencken, Samuel Eliot Morison, Harold Laski, Heywood Broun, Frieda Kirchwey, Maxwell Anderson, John Dos Passos, and Edmund Wilson were just a few of the people who became entangled in the case and wrote about it.

There is still a question in the minds of many judges and lawyers as to the guilt of Sacco and Vanzetti. It is certainly one of the least satisfactory cases ever to have appeared before the American bar. Robert's testimony went into the voluminous histories of the case, along with the millions of words containing the testimony of others.

Some time later, Benchley must have had this frustration in mind when he wrote about an imaginary trial. By then he was more objective and could even see humor in the situation:

"Newspaper accounts of trials always bring out the cleverest in me. They induce daydreams in which I am the witness on the stand" (here's Walter Mitty on the stand, before Thurber conceived him) "and if you don't know some of my imaginary comebacks to an imaginary cross examiner you have missed some of the most stimulating reading in the history of American jurisprudence.

"These little reveries usually take place after I have read the transcript of a trial, while I am on a long taxi ride or seated at a desk with plenty of other work to do. The knowledge that I have completely floored my adversary and the imaginary congratulations of my friends (also imaginary) seem more worthwhile than any amount of fiddling work to be done.

"During these cross-questionings I am always very calm—in a nice way that is—never cocky. However frantic my inquisitor may wax, I just sit there burning him up with each answer, winning the admiration of the courtroom, and at times even a smile from the judge himself." (He didn't get much of a smile from Fuller.) "At the end of my examination the judge is crazy about me.

"Just what the trial is about I never get quite clear in my mind. Sometimes the subject changes in the middle of the questioning, to allow for the insertion of an especially good crack on my part. I don't think I'm ever actually the defendant, although I don't know why I should feel that I am immune from trial by a jury of my peers—if such exist.

". . . I step down from the stand, fresh as a daisy, there is a round of applause which the court makes no attempt to silence. In fact, I have known certain judges to wink pleasantly at me as I take my seat." (Certainly not Judge Thayer.) "Judges are only human after all. My only fear is that, if I am ever really called upon to testify in court, I won't be asked the right questions."

During Benchley's career as drama critic for *Life* magazine, every first-nighter became familiar with his laugh. It was perhaps the most authentic laugh ever born. No would-be humorist could find an easier mark. A joke like, "We have three children and my wife doesn't want to have another one because I read that every fourth child born into the world is a Chinese" could break Robert up. That laugh would so pervade the theater that sometimes even the actors would have to stop and shiver with private, responsive mirth. Ethel Barrymore, of all people, was particularly susceptible to it.

Perhaps Benchley's most quoted remark during a premiere occurred on the evening *The Squall* opened at the 48th Street Theater on Broadway. Blanche Yurka was the star and the story dealt with peasants who spoke in a mysterious broken English. A gypsy girl came on stage and crawled to the feet of a matriarch and kissed the hem of her dress.

"Me Nubi," said the gypsy girl. "Nubi good girl. Nubi stay."

Robert got up. "Me bad boy," he said. "Me Bobby. Me go." And he left the theater.

Anybody who ever saw Robert around town in those days knew that he always carried with him a smart looking natural-leather bag. Benchley called it his Noah bag. It was designed by Robert's friend, Gerald Murphy, who was then the president of Mark Cross, a store noted for its fine leather products.

The idea of the Noah bag was born at Longchamps

Race Track in Paris. Robert and Gerald Murphy were at the races together, and Robert noticed a jockey dismounting from his horse carrying a feedbag on one arm. He decided that the feedbag would be a perfect thing for Mark Cross to sell. The "Noah bag" was so called because Robert said it looked like the sort of thing that Noah would have taken into the ark with him. He used one constantly for papers, passport, gifts or anything else and gave it as presents to people who pleased him—and so many did.

Benchley, along with dozens of writers and artists of the twenties, found Gerald and Sara Murphy perfect companions.

The Murphys, a generation before the phrase was coined, were the beautiful people. They were the real thing, with breeding, money, looks, charm, taste, and intelligence. They owned a legendary house in Antibes, purchased after a visit to Cole Porter (one of Gerald's classmates at Yale) who loved the southern French coast and had his own place there. The Murphy house was a villa on a hill below a lighthouse. The previous owner had imported almost every known shrub and tree to create a flower-filled garden borrowed from Xanadu.

The Murphys had a flat sunroof on the villa, in place of the usual slanting top and they built an outdoor terrace of gray and white marble tile. Anticipating a furniture craze of several decades to come, they ordered rattan chairs and marble-topped tables for the terrace.

Inside, the villa's color scheme was stark black and white; black satin furniture, white walls and fresh flowers everywhere.

They couldn't abide large parties and gave small ones so that the guests could speak freely. The guests represented the avant-garde of all art forms: Picasso, Stravinsky, Diaghilev, Hemingway, Fitzgerald, Dos Passos—and, one summer, the Robert Benchleys.

Gertrude and Robert lived in a stable that the Murphys had converted into a complete, charming cottage. It was in the midst of an orange grove and was called "Ferme des Orangers." Benchley rechristened it "La Ferme Derangée."

That summer the Benchleys saw a lot of Mrs. Parker and the Scott Fitzgeralds as well as their hosts. There was a magic chemistry about the Fitzgerald-Murphy foursome. In spite of no interests in common, they were devoted friends. The Murphys responded to art, literature, ballet, and the theater. The Fitzgeralds weren't interested in any of this. According to Gerald Murphy, Scott Fitzgerald cared for little else in the world but Zelda, his work and his own neuroses. Oddly, in that sun-soaked portion of the world, the Riviera, Scott Fitzgerald chose not to lose his pallor. He watched others basking under the hot Mediterranean sky, but never would stay still long enough to tan his own white skin.

Dorothy Parker was given a cottage by the Murphys named La Bastide, meaning a small country house. Years later, when she was married to Alan Campbell,

Mrs. Parker told him of an incident witnessed by herself, the Murphys and the Benchleys; Campbell used it
as the basis of a "casual" for the back-of-the-book
section of *The New Yorker*. Campbell's story deals
with a man (Fitzgerald) who has a reputation for being
colorful. Attending the theater with some friends, he sees
on the sidewalk a woman selling nuts and candies from a
flat tray suspended on a long strap hung round her neck.
Suddenly the man kicks the tray. The little objects on it
go flying all over the place, the man's friends stare un-
believingly at the disaster, and the man realizes belatedly
that he has offended everyone. He hands the woman a
twenty-dollar bill . . . Obviously, it isn't enough nor
could anything have been enough to excuse the incident.

The story was based on the odd and juvenile kind of
humor with which Scott Fitzgerald was cursed. (And
"cursed" is the only possible word considering the
ultracivilized perspectives of his friends.) There was the
time he tried to dislodge a shaky chair leg from under
one of the Murphy guests. Philip Barry called, "Oh, for
God's sake, Scott, get up from there and stop crawling
around!" Then there was his inability to grasp the
pleasantries of Gerald Murphy and Benchley. Yet there
is so much empathy and humor in Fitzgerald's books
that these gaucheries seem like fables about another
person living inside Fitzgerald.

Summer evenings on the terrace Benchley and Murphy
used to argue about the French with another Murphy
guest, Monty Woolley (who later became famous as

Sheridan Whiteside, the character modeled after Alexander Woollcott in *The Man Who Came to Dinner*). Benchley and Murphy were Francophiles; Woolley thought anything Gallic was absurd. Finally Murphy pinned him down.

"Monty, just what is it you don't like about the French, with their marvelous food and wines and art . . . how can you find anything to *dis*like?"

"I'll tell you what I dislike," said Woolley. "The trouble with the French is that they sit around twenty-four hours a day talking *French*."

Like Benchley, Gerald Murphy had intuitive, swift politeness—a trait bestowed on the character Dick Diver in the early section of Fitzgerald's *Tender Is the Night*. And, also like Benchley, Murphy could evoke the absolute best in anyone; people flowered in his presence.

The Murphys were understandably upset when it became apparent that Fitzgerald had used them as the prototypes of Nicole and Dick Diver. They were even angrier when the fictional couple changed personalities mid-book and became the Fitzgeralds in a state of disintegration. In spite of this feeling, the Murphys stuck by the Fitzgeralds and helped them in every possible way—emotionally, personally, financially, and artistically—until the very end. It was the same sort of unquestioned devotion that Benchley awarded his friends: if you cared about someone, it didn't really matter how many mistakes he made or how foolish he seemed to others; it was up to you to help him.

# CHAPTER TEN

# "The Pigeons
# Are Going to Win"

The world of the machine was an alien one for Benchley. He would go to almost any length to avoid dealing with a mechanical object. He preferred to send out for ice rather than grapple with a refrigerator ice tray. He barely learned to drive a car, for he knew and cared nothing about automobiles. Once while talking with friends, the conversation settled on cars: makes, models, years, engines. Somebody turned to Benchley and asked, "What's your car?"

"Red," he answered, quite seriously.

He hated planes; and a tired typewriter ribbon was his despair. Even paper towels could get him down. He wrote: "The question of paper towels has been gone into many times by reformers, but I do not remember ever having seen the specific matter of those two little bits of paper that come off in your fingers the first time you try to pull a paper towel out of its box. They really call for attention. If you happen to be the dreamer type like me, you may stand for hours holding out two bits of paper for somebody to take off your fingers."

"I have now reached an age when I feel that I am pretty well able to take care of myself against animate enemies. By 'animate enemies' I mean living people, like burglars, drunks, or police—people who set out with a definite idea in their minds of getting me. Mind you, I don't mean that I can lick these people in a hand-to-hand encounter, but I do know, in a general way, what to do when they attack me, even if it is only to run.

"It is the inanimate enemies who have me baffled. The hundred and one bits of wood and metal that go to make up the impedimenta of our daily life—the shoes and pins, the picture books and door keys, the bits of fluff and sheets of newspaper—each and every one with just as much vicious ill will toward me personally as the meanest footpad who roams the streets, each and every one bent on my humiliation and working together, as on one great team, to bedevil and confuse me and to get me into a neurasthenics' home before I am sixty. I can't fight these boys. They've got me licked."

The mechanics of certain social situations also baffled him. In the following paragraphs he dealt fearlessly with a delicate human predicament that has all too little seen the light of day; what to do "when you find that both your right hand and your left hand partner are busily engaged in conversation with somebody else. . . . you can always make believe that you are talking to the person opposite, making little conversational faces and sounds into thin air, nodding your head yes or no, and laughing politely every now and then. This may fool your hostess but it's going to confuse the person sitting opposite you in case he or she happens to catch your act. You can always get busily at work on the nuts in front of your plate, arranging them on the tablecloth in fancy patterns . . . if you have thought to bring along a bit of charcoal, you can draw little pictures on the back of the lady on either side of you, or you might start smothering the nicer looking back with kisses. This would at least get one of your partners to turn around."

Telephones were part of the plot, too. "When I am called by a secretary" he said, "who doesn't tell me who's calling but says, 'wait a minute,' and then goes off somewhere for five minutes, I hang up."

He claimed that his white suit in the summer looked much whiter than anybody else's white suit; he thought perhaps it was because he hadn't put it on right. When he was wearing this white suit, and saw somebody coming toward him, he'd be very self-conscious about it. As soon as the person came within earshot, Benchley would explain: "It's white."

As for evening wear, he called himself a "bender." He said it corresponded to "a bleeder in the medical world. One touch and my shirt front bends. By the end of the evening I am lucky if it is still buttoned and covering any portion of my chest."

Benchley's side in his own war scored whenever he discovered "a good unreliable dentist. To have a dentist's secretary call up and say, 'Doctor Murch is staying home today and won't be able to keep that appointment'—does life offer any more satisfactory thrill?"

For most of his life Benchley was a bird hater. He said he understood how St. Francis could be very fond of birds, but he himself had more of a feeling for dogs. In one of his pieces he struck out savagely at pigeons:

"Although I live in the middle of a very large city, I am awakened every morning by a low gargling sound which turns out to be the result of one, two, or three pigeons walking in at my window and sneering at me. . . . There is something more than just a passing criticism in these birds making remarks about me. They have some ugly scheme afoot against me, and I know it. Sooner or later it will come out, and then I can sue.

"This thing has been going on ever since I was in college. In our college everybody was very proud of the pigeons. I was decent enough to them in my undergraduate days; I let them walk up and down my back and tried to be as nice as I could without actually letting them see that I wasn't so crazy about it.

"But somehow the word got around in pigeon circles that Benchley was anti-bird. At 6:30 in the morning the parade would begin. The line of march was as follows: light on Benchley's windowsill, march once in through the open window, going grumble, grumble, grumble in a sinister tone, then out and stand on the sill,

urging other pigeons to come in and take a crack at
it. . . .

"I have been known to take in dogs who were
obviously impostors and put them through college. I am
a sucker for kittens, even though I know that one day
they will grow into cats who will betray me. I have
even been known to pat a tiger cub, which accounts
for my writing this article with my left hand. But as
far as pigeons go, I am through. It is a war to the death
and I have a horrible feeling that the pigeons are going
to win."

He claimed there was a bloodthirsty bird who would
sit outside his window and threaten him—not a pigeon,
just a bloodthirsty, anonymous songbird. And there
were two guinea hens "like drunken townies hanging
around the corner drugstore. They annoyed me with
remarks, then actually set in motion and tried to trip me
up . . . I asked Dr. Le Noix, an eminent French scientist
who happens to be sleeping across the foot of my bed
this morning, about it . . . and he says we must be
careful not to credit the little winged fellows with intelligence when they behave in what seems like an intelligent manner."

Benchley hated parlor games. As soon as people at
parties got around to Twenty Questions or anything
else that they considered good, intellectual fun, Benchley
would walk out. He said, "In the exclusive set (no
diphtheria cases allowed) in which I travel, I am known
as a heel in the matter of parlor games. I am usually not

included in *any* game that can be planned in advance. If
people foresee an evening of 'Consequences' coming
over them, they whisper 'get Benchley out of the house.
Get him a horse to ride or some beads to string—anything to get him out of the way.' For, I forgot to tell
you, not only am I a non-participant in parlor games,
but I am a militant non-participant. I heckle from the
sidelines. I throw stones and spit at the players. Hence
the nickname: 'Sweet Old Bob,' or sometimes just the
initials."

In spite of Benchley's own feeling about word games,
he did respect the ingenuity of others. Once during a
session with Frank Sullivan and Patricia Collinge, somebody said, "Use the word 'disintegrate' in a sentence."
It wasn't half a minute before Miss Collinge replied,
"Disintegrate day for de Irish," as indeed it immediately
was in Benchley's opinion.

In the midst of affliction, there were always certain
small satisfactions. "For example," he wrote, "I derive
sensual pleasure from lifting off a milk bottle cap with
some small pointed instrument like a pin, especially if it
resists just a bit around the edges. I find the greatest
thrill is experienced when the cap is exactly half off, but
the final release is worth waiting for. There is a minor
excitement in pressing the cap back on, especially if it
has not become bent during the removal.

"Unwrapping the tinfoil from a piece of cream cheese
furnishes a tactile pleasure of a high order which is
marred only by the difficulty of getting it all off. Executed slowly and carefully, however, the satisfaction

from the first two-thirds of the wrapping process makes up for the anticlimax of having to pick out the remaining bits of tinfoil with a fork. I have often been reduced to the point of swooning by the sensation of holding a book of just the right size and smoothness in my right hand. A pocket edition, about 4½" by 6½", printed in 10-point Goudy and possibly 250 pages thick, is a delight to hold and gaze at, even though it be written in an unfamiliar language. In the same class I would place a fresh copy of a well printed Sunday newspaper before it has been torn apart by the women of the family. Among other nice things to hold in the right hand are the butt of a Colt automatic (preferably un-loaded), the warm bowl of a pipe, a round cake of soap, and a smooth stone held in position for skipping across the surface of a pond. The sight of the stone skipping is not bad either."

Even stronger than his feeling against inanimate ene-mies was his hatred for exercise. "Exercise," he said to his friend Jock Whitney, "is a form of nervous disorder."

Benchley did swim, and he and Gertrude had played quite a bit of tennis since they were in high school together. Gertrude claims that she was the better player, but never won because Bob always made her laugh. Undeniably, the form of exercise Benchley most en-joyed, was lying down on that couch in his living room at the Royalton.

# CHAPTER ELEVEN

# "There Are Some Men Here
# to Flood the Bed"

What with pigeons, machines and other perils, Benchley decided he needed a secretary. It was a very businesslike decision, but there was nothing businesslike about the way he found his secretary or the way his secretary conducted the Benchley *fonds de commerce*. Robert didn't bother with an employment agency or want ads; he trusted to fate. One rainy day in front of the New York Public Library, he ran into a friend of his who was with a little man named MacGregor. MacGregor had a package with him and Benchley asked MacGregor what it was. MacGregor replied, "Oh, I'm just taking these flowers to a shirt in the shirt hospital."

MacGregor explained that the shirt in the shirt hospital was not really seriously ill—only a minor operation was needed: the cuffs were being turned. Robert said he understood very well, but pointed out that as far as he was concerned there were too many shirt hospitals all over the place and he knew several art galleries which were fronts for shirt hospitals.

This knowing exchange convinced Benchley that MacGregor was the ideal secretary. An arrangement was made whereby MacGregor would show up at the Royalton every day, look at the checkbook, get Benchley out of bed, and perform other odd jobs. Sometimes MacGregor would open the day by shaking Benchley and announcing, "There are some men here to flood the bed for skating." Life with MacGregor was not dull.

MacGregor never slept, a habit which Benchley respected and probably envied. Benchley used MacGregor as the hero in several pieces:

"What's the news this morning, Mr. MacGregor," I asked, peeking around from behind a hangover. " 'Just give me the key words.' 'It says here,' replied MacGregor catering to my whim, 'that the Don Cossacks who have been exiled in this country since the Russian Revolution are going to elect a new Ataman this month.' 'I know why you read me that item in quotes,' I countered, 'so that you could say At-A-Man!'

MacGregor blushed furiously.

" 'Go ahead and say it anyway,' I said, my generous side coming to the fore.

" 'At-A-Man!' murmured MacGregor, making believe he had not said it."

Or, when Benchley explained the Indian rope trick he

mentions that "while in India, a friend of mine, a Mr. MacGregor, assisted me in confusing the natives in more ways than one. We dressed up in Indian costume, for one thing. This confused even us, but we took it good naturedly.

". . . Mirabile dictu. Mr. MacGregor disappeared into thin air and *drew the rope up after him.* Even I had to look twice. It was a stupendous victory. 'Are there any questions?' I asked the mob.

"'What is Clark Gable like?' someone said.

"'He's a very nice fellow,' I answered. 'Modest and unassuming. I see quite a lot of him when I am in Hollywood. . . .'

"It wasn't until I got back to our New York office that I saw Mr. MacGregor again, and I forgot to ask him how he ever got down."

On a trip to Bermuda once during a hurricane, MacGregor and Benchley were the only two on ship who weren't violently ill. They took turns putting on shows for each other, one playing the part of audience by smoking a big black cigar.

After many years of honorable service, MacGregor died of a heart attack. It turned out that many of the papers that had belonged to Benchley, including a great many of the pieces written for *Vanity Fair* during the '20s were lost in a fire that had ravaged MacGregor's Bermuda house. The material was never found—why it was there at all is one of the enigmas of the MacGregor Story.

Sometimes Benchley would travel to Europe in the summer with his family, or sometimes with his friends: Whitney, Mrs. Parker, Marc Connelly, Douglas Fairbanks, Sr., or John Gilbert. He carried his own atmosphere wherever he went.

Once when Benchley and Douglas Fairbanks were traveling together, Mary Pickford sent an urgent telegram: COME HOME AT ONCE, and Fairbanks, the swashbuckler, meekly took the next boat back.

Another time in Paris, Benchley noted that his companion, John Gilbert, looked morose. Benchley asked him why he was sulking. Gilbert had just been going through an unhappy love affair with Greta Garbo; he had tried to reach her in Sweden, but she wouldn't come to the phone.

"John," said Bob, "why don't you reach for a Lucky instead of a Swede?"

Robert decided to take Jennie, now nearly eighty, along on one of his European trips. Jennie was all for it, and wrote Robert to find out whether she should bring her bicycle along when she visited her niece and nephew in Paris. Robert loved having Jennie with him, but he wasn't quite sure how to break the news to her that he was no longer a Dry.

On board ship Robert ordered crème de menthe and told Jennie that it was medicine for his digestion. He let her smell it. She smelled, but did not taste, and from that time on Robert ordered only colorless drinks, such as gin, vodka or cointreau. One evening, before he'd had a chance to order a drink, Jennie reminded him that

he'd forgotten his digestion medicine. He thanked her
very much and ordered a vodka. Something must have
tipped Jennie off, though, because a little while later she
asked Gertrude if Robert ever drank. Gertrude was
evasive and suggested that she ask Robert.

"I wouldn't insult him with the question," said Jennie.
She was adhering to her own mysterious code of eti-
quette and ethics. Her major dread was scene-making.
She had a litany that she used during times of trouble,
"I refuse to reflect a disturbance, I refuse to reflect a
disturbance." She once told Gertrude that it came in
very handy when a man rang the doorbell just as Jennie
had reached a crucial moment in doughnut-frying. She
heard the insistent peal, waited, heard it again, wiped
her floury hands on her apron, and opened the door to
a salesman who (probably for the first time in his
career) was greeted by: "I refuse to reflect a disturbance!"

The following summer Benchley went to Paris with
John Hay Whitney and Nicholas Ludington. Whitney
always booked an extra cabin for any friend who happened to come along. The three of them rented a suite
at the Crillon, with a terrace. Benchley, who could never
resist a balcony, appeared as he had at the time of
Sherwood's party in New York, to deliver a message
to his public. He bowed as a few people in the street
began to clap, and made a speech in halting Italian that
amounted to: "Passengers will refrain from using the
washroom while the train is not in motion." He repeated
this with varying inflections as the crowd applauded.

Wherever he traveled, Benchley tended to miss New England food. He was particularly fond of steamed clams. Once, in "21," Benchley asked the captain if steamed clams were on the menu. He was told no, not that night, please try tomorrow. This was a family party, and the Benchleys returned the next day, had their clams, but were not charged for them—the captain had dug them himself to please the Benchleys.

Benchley loved to stay at the best hotels and was known far and wide as a big tipper. During a brief stay at a hotel in Paris, however, he found that he was not getting the sort of service he wanted. When he left the hotel, the doorman sprang to attention (for the first time) to open the door of a taxi and hold out his hand. Benchley just looked at him.

"You're not going to forget me, sir?" said the door-man.

Benchley seized his hand and shook it vigorously. "No," he said. "I'll write you every day."

And of course there was the famous time in Hollywood when Benchley left the Trocadero, found it was raining, and turned to a resplendently garbed, mauve-faced gentleman and said, "Call me a taxi."

"I beg your pardon sir," said the resplendently garbed, mauve-faced gentleman, "but I happen to be Admiral So-and-So of the United States Navy."

"O.K." said Robert, "in that case, call me a battle-ship."

Benchley often complained that the dozens of telephone calls he received every day at the Royalton were a distraction in his work. He asked the telephone operator, who may be called Daisy, to screen the calls. The arrangement worked out satisfactorily and an actor friend of Benchley's, also living at the Royalton, evolved a similar contract with Daisy, who was only too pleased to perform any service for so handsome a man. Then the actor met a splendid lady who pleased him very much; so much, in fact, that he decided he could not conduct any respectable rendezvous with her at the Royalton, with its bleak furnishings and Victorian aspect. He decided to take her to the Plaza, and she was to telephone him for traffic instruction during the day. Unfortunately, the actor got very drunk and woke at the Plaza later that night to find that the other occupant of the bed in his palatial suite was Daisy, who had screened all his calls only too well that day, including the one from the splendid lady explaining she was unable to keep their appointment.

Maybe the phone calls, the friendships, the night-life kept Benchley from writing the Queen Anne book; or maybe not. Friends pointed out that if he'd gone to an analyst there might have been no nonsense about the Queen Anne book, and his private life might have been simpler. But it wouldn't have worked out, really. Benchley had a deep distrust of psychiatry. Once he said, "the derivation of one color from the mixture of two other colors is not generally considered a sexual phenomenon, but that is because the psychoanalysts haven't gotten around to it yet."

Somehow, in the world of the arts in the 1920s and

'30s, critics didn't take up nearly as much room as they do today. It seemed much easier for writers to create instead of relying for publicity on pieces about each other. As Robert Graves points out, "Some people call this a critical, as opposed to a creative, age. I doubt that it is either. The criticism racket . . . is as bankrupt as the poetry racket." Some of the American authors of the period were Sherwood Anderson, Willa Cather, Hemingway, Fitzgerald, Lardner, Faulkner, Dos Passos, Sinclair Lewis, Theodore Dreiser, Conrad Aiken, Edith Wharton, and Eugene O'Neill. Critics still hadn't learned how to turn ten words into a thousand words: a book review in *Life* magazine would often be very short as well as very informative. In one issue, Arnold Bennett's novel, *Riceyman's Steps* and Rose Macaulay's novel, *A Tale Told by an Idiot*, were both reviewed in about half a page. The critic, Diana Warwick, recognized the worth of the books and managed to convey it to readers economically and modestly.

Benchley respected the English language, a point of view which seems to sit on the other side of the see-saw from fatuity. Recently a well-known drama reviewer in New York wrote as an entire sentence, "Besides laughing, I thought it was pathetically brave." Another critic wrote, ". . . all criticism is an effort at self-integration . . ." Benchley might have found it puzzling to think of somebody committing an act of self-integration: "Dr. Jekyll, meet Mr. Hyde?"

Benchley isn't around today to wince over the excesses that pass under the name of intelligent literary criticism, but we can envision how he might have suffered by rereading a piece he wrote in the 1930s, when, as a man who treasured good sense, perspective, talent and judgment, he was appalled to read some of the pretentious nonsense that even then was being heeded by the Eternal Band of Determined Serious Readers:

DISCOVERING WEBER AND FIELDS
*If There Had Been Erudite Criticism in the Nineties*

From the lowly precincts of the music halls has arisen a new pair of pragmatists. The names that appear on the bills are Weber and Fields, but the hands are the hands of William James.

The method of these zanies is eclectic. From Zeno the Stoic they have taken the doctrine of "six-times-six-is-thirty-six." From Anaxagoras the theory that the Whole is less than any of its parts. From Francis Bacon the denial of Truth as a substantive. From L.G.B. three dozen woolen stockings and a crate of oranges.

Take for example the scene where *Mike* and *Meyer* are discussing occupations (in itself pure dialectics):

MEYER: Vot are you doing?
MIKE: Voiking in a nut factory.
MEYER: Doing vot?
MIKE: Nutting.
MEYER: Sure—but vot are you *doing?*
MIKE: Nutting.
MEYER: I know, but vot voik are you doing?
MIKE: Nutting, I tole you.
MEYER: (*poking his finger in Mike's eye*): Ou-u-u-u, how I lofe you!

Here we have the new philosophy of the subconscious,

the stirrings of a new American humor which derives from the modern German school of Merkwurdigkeit, or Es-giebt-also-es-ist. In the American mind is being born, through the medium of the music hall, a consciousness of national social satire which bids fair to revolutionize thought on this side of the Atlantic. Could a better example be found than the following dialogue between these two super-clowns in their latest show:

MIKE: (*referring to offstage noises*) A soldier has been shot.

MEYER: Vere vos he shot?

MIKE: In de eggcitement!

Here, in these words, lies America. The America of today, with its flaring gas lights, its thundering cable cars, the clatter of its hansoms, and the deafening whistle of its peanut stands. The young, vibrant spirit of America, locked in the message of two clowns! And, with the coming of jazz, twenty years from now, we shall see the full expression of the young nation's strivings toward the Greater Smooch.

# CHAPTER TWELVE

# "I've Tried to Worry
# but I Can't"

Benchley and Harold Ross, the founder of *The New Yorker* magazine, were good friends and saw each other often at the Round Table. In 1927, Benchley joined Ross's organization as writer of a column called the Wayward Press. In 1929 he became *The New Yorker*'s drama editor. In those days the magazine's editorial offices were at 25 West 45th Street. It was an old building and Benchley was impressed by the unusual aspect of the men's room, where the customary ratio of stand-up and sit-down facilities was reversed.

Ross was supposed by some to be a tiger, but Benchley's relationship with him was excellent. (Gertrude was the only person who ever called Ross "Harold.") Ross respected talent above everything else in the world. The

fact that copy might occasionally be late or not turn
up at all didn't interfere with his pride in his authors
and editors. Ross recognized Benchley as somebody su-
premely right for a magazine with high standards of
quality, good taste, accuracy. "*Not* for the old lady
in Dubuque," said the first promotion piece circulated
by Ross, and, after a slow start, the empire was established. With England's *Puck* and the old *Life* as its
preceptors, *The New Yorker* flourished. Its core of
detached, civilized humor—plus the best copy-editing
in the world—made it a joy and a necessity to anyone
with taste.

This was the time of the giants of American humor:
Lardner, Thurber, Benchley, Sullivan, White, Perelman;
it was a period like the early nineteenth century in
England when lyric poetry bloomed, producing Shelley,
Keats, Byron, Wordsworth, a happy accident of gifted
creators meeting public appreciation.

*Punch* recently circulated a letter referring to the lack
of sophisticated humor in the world today. It has certainly been missing in America lately, but for more
than three decades *The New Yorker* did its best to bring
the most talented humorists of their time to an enthusiastic world. Perhaps, as has been the case with fashions
in dress and in other branches of literature, the pendulum
will swing again and the tasteless comedy now in vogue
will disappear as thoroughly in the near future as another
kind of vulgarity did once before in the nineteen twenties

when *Life* and *The New Yorker* annihilated the dull, manufactured joke.

One of *The New Yorker* editors whose career started in those early days recalls that the copy desk had a code name for Benchley: Uncle Bob. "Has Uncle Bob's copy come in yet?" "No, of course not," was the usual exchange. The copy was predictably late and accompanied by separate and elaborate alibis. During one hectic waiting period, this editor decided to forget his worries at "21." He had just received a telephone call from Uncle Bob, in which it was claimed Uncle was dead or out-of-town or both. The editor was not startled but disturbed to see Benchley at the other end of the bar in "21," the center of a gay group of friends. Benchley spotted him, fingered his tie nervously—then invited the editor to join him. The evening wore on at "21" and later at an after-hours club; there was no copy handed in that night.

Ross had told his staff that Benchley's complicated alibis were mainly an attempt to pacify that Puritan conscience; still, the copy desk was not always able to understand Uncle Bob's excuses. For instance, the week when every literate person on the Eastern seaboard knew that Benchley was to be best man at the Whitney-Altemus wedding, the editors were *hurt* to receive a call from Uncle. He said his typewriter had just been stolen and he was phoning from a pay station. In the background could be clearly heard the strains of a large orchestra and various bachelor-party voices.

When at length the copy was delivered it was, as al-

ways, immaculate, single-spaced on yellow paper, beau-
tifully typed, needing almost no editing, with oddly
designed margins conceived by Benchley with the
thought that, if he left almost no room on the left,
editors wouldn't mess around with corrections.

Readers of the magazine somehow shared a mental
composite picture of a *New Yorker* writer: totally
urbane, charming, witty, talented, self-effacing. Benchley
was the personification of it.

Nowadays it is the fashion for humorists to talk
seriously about themselves at great length in interviews.
One said recently that the "put-down era" is "ready for
me. I make fun of sacred cows, I make fun of authority.
I'm the guy who tells the boss off and gets away with
it. The time is right for me."

The people who were associated with *The New
Yorker* style of humor in the '20s and '30s would have
turned away unhappily at the sound of these words.
Once a man decides how very funny he is and how
essential he is to civilization, his charm as a humorist
seems to evaporate. Benchley modestly declined involve-
ment with cosmic thoughts about the meaning of humor
or the fate of mankind. When someone asked him about
his stand on the future of the race, Benchley replied,
"I've tried to worry, but I can't . . ."

When Robert took over The *New Yorker*'s dramatic
criticism from Charles Brackett, he enjoyed opening
nights more than ever. The first review of his that
appeared in the magazine was the week of September

14, 1929. The play was called *They're Off* and it was "a gem of bad taste." As for *Sweet Adeline*, Benchley said, "it's not without its dull stretches, and when they are dull they are *good* and dull." But his friend Charles Butterworth was in it; and Helen Morgan, "an excessively lush personality," pleased him. Robert also found, that September, that he preferred Ibsen (*The Wild Duck*) to Chekhov (*The Sea Gull*).

In October 1929, Robert covered *June Moon* written by his idol, Ring Lardner, and George S. Kaufman. Robert said he found it great. "You can't laugh and write too, though," so he decided not to write about it. He added that everybody has to write a play with George S. Kaufman sometime, or the state won't license it.

About the *Playboy of the Western World*, he wrote, "It's not a tough job to undertake, but the Irish Players don't do it well. To talk with a brogue is their chief professional asset."

Benchley said that he was thinking of having personal stationery engraved with something the *Herald Tribune* critic had said about him: "Mr. Benchley's guffaws rising as sort of an overtone over the general merriment make my evening complete."

Benchley found fault with the 1930 production of Shaw's *The Apple Cart*. He thought it was a dramatized pamphlet and asked, "Why need we be bored?" When Benchley reviewed a movie written by Shaw, *How He Lied to Her Husband*, he wrote, "Shaw has forgotten all he ever knew about the theater. All we have left

is a bust of the noble brow and beard." He raved over
*The Green Pastures,* finding it "excellent propaganda
for the Christian Church." His friend, Marc Connelly,
was its Pulitzer Prize-winning author.

As for *The Rivals* he said, "of course you know the
charming spirited old comedy? Well, it's just as dull
as any other eighteenth-century comedy." About *Uncle
Vanya:* ". . . stalks with majestic simplicity through a
gloomy old house. . . ." Benchley felt that the production left him waiting for some sensitive Stranger to
come up and press his hand murmuring, "I understand,
I understand."

Benchley complained that there were too many dirty
wisecracks that year in plays, but he did like *Lysistrata,*
finding it, "frankly and openly a comedy of sex, and by
its very frankness and openness, quite clean."

This was quite a revealing statement. Benchley didn't
mind anything that was frank; what he hated was fur-
tiveness, leering, and the idea that a long, dirty joke
could be made into an acceptable work of literature or
theater. The successes of the 1960s, with so many leers
and so little substance, would have horrified him A decline of taste was for him a decline of civilization.

In 1930 there was a production of *The Third Garrick
Gaieties,* but Benchley found it not so good as the first
two.

He approved of a comedian named Jack Benny who
was in Earl Carroll's *Vanities,* saying, "Mr. Benny has
long been a weakness of this department."

27. "Tomorrow I purpose to regulate my room."

-DR. SAMUEL JOHNSON

28. Lunch at the famous Algonquin Round Table. Cast of characters, beginning left foreground and moving clockwise: Robert E. Sherwood, Dorothy Parker, Robert Benchley, Alexander Woollcott, Heywood

Broun, Marc Connelly, Frankiln P. Adams, Edna Ferber, George S. Kaufman. At the back: Lynn Fontanne, Alfred Lunt, Frank Crownin-shield and Frank Case. (Drawing by Al Hirschfeld.)

29. The Algonquin by one who has heard all about it.

30. Mr. and Mrs. John Hay Whitney at Belmont Park in 1935. The former Elizabeth Altemus is now Mrs. Cloyce Tippett.

31 & 32. Early Benchleyana from the *Harvard Lampoon*.

33. The Robert Sherwood-Mary Brandon wedding party. Top row left to right: the groom, Robert Benchley, Frank Case (fifth from left), Alexander Woollcott (profile), Grant Mitchell, John Emerson. Middle row: the bride, Margalo Gillmore (fourth from left), Marc Connelly, Douglas Fairbanks.

In September of 1930 Benchley saw a play by Marya
Mannes called *Cafe: A Play of the Boulevards*. Benchley said, "It's pretty thin—even the man selling dirty
postcards didn't seem real."

His friend Ernest Hemingway's *A Farewell to Arms*
was made into a play but Benchley pointed out that
the book was obviously *not* a play. As for Kaufman
and Hart's *Once in a Lifetime*, he wrote, "Somebody's
blood has gone into the making of *Once in a Lifetime*,
which is why it is so much more than a comedy."

The year 1930 was a good one for the theater. *Three's
a Crowd* with Clifton Webb, Fred Allen, and Libby
Holman opened, and Benchley pointed out, "Here we
have the same triumvirate as in the *First Little Show*,
if Miss Libby Holman doesn't mind being called a *vir*
for a minute." This was typical of Benchley's penchant
for accuracy. He couldn't even stand changing Libby
Holman's gender for the sake of a quotable phrase
about a play. He loved the production and said that
Howard Dietz had "one of the few civilized senses of
humor on Broadway today."

Years later, Howard Dietz was to reply in kind after
Benchley's death . . . "Mr. Benchley goes down in history as the most lovable, loyal and companionable person, mourned almost every day by his friends . . . I
should like to add, for the record, that, among other
sacred things, I consider him the wisest man I have
ever known."

The point was, they both meant it, and they were both right.

It was also the year that Benchley made his proclamation: "I am now definitely ready to state that sex as a theatrical property . . . is tiresome . . . I am sick of rebellious Youth."

At the end of 1930 Benchley wrote in one of his columns, "I would like to protest the killing by a taxicab, on December 10th, of Wesley Hill, the Angel Gabriel of *Green Pastures* . . . There was really no sense in that, Lord, and you know it as well as I do."

Early in 1931 Benchley saw his beloved W. C. Fields in *Ballyhoo*, and Arthur Byron in a play called *Five Star Final* by Louis Weitzenkorn. "'At's hittin' 'em, Mr. Weitzenkorn-boy!" wrote Mr. Benchley, showing his approval of the script.

On February 21, 1931, there was a drama piece headed "Kindly Accept Substitutes." It was by Mr. Benchley's friend, Mrs. Parker, who was filling in for the master while he was off in Hollywood making movie shorts.

Mrs. Parker was in her usual form. She called herself the only one who didn't find *The Barretts of Wimpole Street* even a *good* play. She said she paid it the tribute of tears, but that that meant nothing because she wept at the sight of any Victorian costume or at a rendition of Mighty Lak' a Rose. Mrs. Parker said she did admire Katharine Cornell, she did admire the sets and the costumes—in fact, the only thing she didn't like about *The Barretts of Wimpole Street* was the play.

Mrs. Parker had an odd personal dislike for Lorenz

Hart, the brilliant lyricist who worked with Richard Rodgers. She found his rhymes annoying and deplored their "nastiness of flavor." She demanded to know "whatever became of that little thing called taste" in a musical called *America's Sweetheart* (which by today's standards would seem a paragon of wholesomeness). At the end of that particular column, Mrs. Parker had a note, "Mr. Benchley: Please come home. Nothing is forgiven."

Mrs. Parker mentioned that her dearest dreads in a play title were the word "yesterday," and transposed adjectives and nouns. It was during this season of filling in for Mr. Benchley that, on the 21st of March, she saw *The House Beautiful* (and wrote her famous phrase: "'The House Beautiful' is for me the play lousy").

Aside from falling asleep at a Shaw revival, *Getting Married*, Mrs. Parker's career as a fill-in dramatic critic was uneventful. Benchley returned from Hollywood in April of '31 to his job and started in with a dissertation beginning, "Life is too long to fret over the Pulitzer Prize."

In June of 1931 he saw *The Bandwagon* with his friends, the Astaires, and a book by Howard Dietz. He defied anyone "to worry about Russian wheat dumping" while this play was going on.

Mr. Benchley wasn't always so ready to praise his friends. When Heywood Broun's play *Shoot the Works*, opened in August of 1931, Benchley wrote, "It has no

more class than a buttercup." His comment on Mae
West in *The Constant Sinner* was, "there is a certain
tough entertainment value in Miss West's dramas, which
might possibly be turned to some good use were it
not for the heavy personality tax it has to bear."
(Through the years this seems to have changed: Miss
West's figure has become more imposing, but her
personality became a good deal lighter.)

In October Benchley wrote, "Broadway has at last
got a fine play for itself, even though it did have to
go back to old August (Smiles) Strindberg for it." It
was Strindberg's *The Father* with Robert Loraine in
the title role.

In November Benchley praised O'Neill's famous tril-
ogy, *Mourning Becomes Electra*. He said that the melo-
drama is "O'Neill's precious inheritance from his
trouper-father. He thrills the bejesus out of us, just as
his father used to do, and that is what we go to the
theater for . . . let's stop talking about the verities and
the unities and take a grand, stupendous play when we
find it and let it go at that."

In November of 1931, Raymond Massey appeared in
Norman Bel Geddes' production of *Hamlet*. Celia
Johnson was Ophelia. Mr. Benchley noted, "Ham is
really an abbreviation for Hamlet."

The Gluyas Williams drawings of Benchley that always appeared in the books were beginning to look
a little stouter and a little more middle-aged. Benchley's

figure had begun to blossom along with his reputation. He was now "Who's Who" material.

An anthologist, asking Robert for an outline of his life, received the following note:

"Since there are fifteen or twenty minutes each day when I have nothing to do, I might as well be writing an autobiography as shaving. . . . material for the first volume has already accumulated and is herewith printed for private circulation. Readers are placed on their honor not to divulge the plot.

"Chapter 1. The first time I ever saw Donald Ogden Stewart he was eating lunch with Edmund Wilson. They were having Yankee pot roast (85¢).

"Chapter 2. I was born September 15, 1889, in Worcester, Massachusetts. I remember that there was a boy in school named George Dixon. Later when I went back to Worcester to get some things I'd left in the attic, I found George had moved and gone to Utica.

"Chapter 3. Chapters from the biography of Mr. Benchley written by his little son, Bobby, at the age of five. 'Daddy is a very funny man, at least he thinks he is. Today he tried to carry some wood up from the cellar to burn in the fireplace and jammed his head against the cellar door.' 'There goes my hand against the door!' he said. Bobby is wrong there. 'What the goddam!' is what I said, although it was the cellar door and it was wood for the fireplace.

"Chapter 5. My grandfather, Henry W. Benchley wore a beard. I never knew him but I've seen pictures of him. Grandmother on my mother's side was a Hey-

ward, although I don't think I ever knew her, either.
The Heywards were quiet and kept to themselves a
great deal. On my father's side everybody was either
a Goddard or a Gale. One of my forebear, I think it
was an Endicott, later had his name changed to Lipsky.
I remember how good baked beans and fish balls used
to taste at Sunday morning breakfasts. . . . I met a man
the other day who said he was Dr. Fischer. 'What Dr.
Fischer?' I asked. *The* Dr. Fischer he replied.

"There was a Dr. Fischer who used to live in Worcester, but I don't think it was he, because that Dr.
Fischer was a woman."

In March of 1932, A. A. Milne (the same Mr. Milne
who made Tonstant Weader fwow up) had a play on
Broadway called *They Don't Mean Any Harm.* Benchley found it rather hard to take. It seemed that a cripple
was to have an operation, and one of the characters
remarked, "It would almost seem ungrateful to God."
Benchley noted, "In other words, don't spoil God's
fun by making Mother able to walk." He added that
this was almost a "burlesque Christianity."

He loved the great Laurette Taylor in any play by
James M. Barrie, but was bored by *Too True to Be
Good* saying, "Shaw really is a Great Man, otherwise
he could not, wearing a full beard, have his picture
taken in a bathing suit."

In February 1933, Benchley had the highest praise for
Noël Coward's *Design for Living,* and he referred to

himself as "having been one of the first to wave a small
flag for the peculiar talents of Miss Tallulah Bankhead."
In November 1933, a musical comedy called *Roberta*
opened. Benchley noted, "A comparative newcomer
to Broadway, Bob Hope, has a slick, humorous delivery
which ought to put him in the front ranks as soon as
he gets something to say which does not bring the
blush of shame to his cheeks."

Later on, when Benchley saw Bob Hope in another
play, he wrote, "For *Roberta*, I threw off an *obiter
dictum* that with better material he would be one of
our best comedians. He is."

All of his life, Benchley admired professional comedians like Hope who could tell a story well and
were experts at timing. They weren't apt to be found
in the Benchley circle of friends, because they were
forced to rely on ready-made jokes, which were taboo
at the Round Table. For example, Benchley admired
Groucho Marx unlimitedly, but remarked to a friend,
"Groucho makes me nervous—he's always on the edge
of the chair." When Benchley was in Hollywood,
however, he and Groucho had a planned meeting and
Groucho must have been more relaxed, because the
two men got along very well indeed.

In December 1933, Benchley found Maxwell Anderson's, *Mary of Scotland*, "fine writing," and he thought
*Tobacco Road*, "has some good, earthy humor"—which
again showed Benchley on the side of frankness about
sex. One of his pet dislikes was Earl Carroll, the producer

of the *Vanities:* Benchley found him in perpetual bad
taste.

Not appearing in *The New Yorker*, but penciled in
on a program for a play called *These Two* in May
1934, Benchley's scrawled notes read, "Hit and run
pregnancy . . . audience of virgins . . . lots of sherry
. . . great strain across room . . ."

About another play at this time, Mr. Benchley remarked that the author was careful to "leave no
stomach unturned."

He expressed his displeasure with what he saw going
on in the world outside the theater with the following
paragraphs:

"Paul Revere leaped into his saddle.

" 'Through every Middlesex village and farm, Bess,
old girl!' he whispered in his mare's ear, and they were
off.

"And, as he rode, the dauntless patriot saw as in a
vision (in fact, it was a vision) the future of the land to
which he was bringing freedom.

"He saw a hundred and ten million people, the men
in derbies, the women in felt hats with little bows on the
top. He saw them pushing one another in and out of
trolley cars on their way to and from work, adding up
figures incorrectly all morning and subtracting them
incorrectly all afternoon, with time out at 12:30 for
frosted chocolates and pimento cheese sandwiches. He
saw fifty million of them trying to prevent the other
sixty million from doing what they wanted to do, and
the sixty million trying to prevent the fifty million from

doing what *they* wanted to do. He saw them all paying taxes to a few hundred of their number for running the government very badly. He saw ten million thin children working and ten thousand fat children playing in the warm sands. And now and again he saw five million youths, cheered on by a hundred million elders with fallen arches, marching out to give their arms and legs and lives for Something to Be Determined Later. And over all he saw the Stars and Stripes fluttering in the artificial breeze of an electric fan operated behind the scenes.

"So tugging at the reins he yelled: 'Whoa, Bess! We're going back to the stable.'"

Some of the woes of the world—shining seas of backed-up cars, air and water pollution, burgeoning populations and mechanical failures—have become more complicated since the heyday of the frosted chocolate, but Benchley's words about taxes and the futility of war might have been written tomorrow.

In 1934 Katharine Hepburn had the misfortune to open in *The Lake*. Mrs. Parker was filling in for Mr. Benchley again, and managed to churn out another immortal line, this time about Miss Hepburn running the gamut of emotions from A to B.

Benchley found Sean O'Casey's *Within the Gates* "a great piece of writing," but warned the producers to watch out for overconfidence.

The word "camp" which lately has enjoyed such strange celebrity was used by Benchley in connection with a show called *Casino Varieties*. He said, "with Gertrude Niesen to sing and the Ritz Brothers to camp, it makes a good evening's entertainment."

On May 12, 1934, he saw his old favorite *Iolanthe*. He chided himself as follows: "After spending wrath on audiences who demand encores, I tried to get third repetitions of 'Thou the Tree and I the Flower.' Why should *any*one applaud *The Mikado* and *Pinafore?* . . . Want to make anything out of it?"

He loved Gilbert and Sullivan, and was a great authority on most of their works. When Mike Todd produced *The Hot Mikado* at the first New York World's Fair in 1939, Benchley took it with a grain of salt and murmured that it was okay to do that to *The Mikado*, which was too popular anyway, but "they better not ever do that to *Iolanthe*."

He really didn't care much for popular music. There was a tune he would always hum from the musical comedy, *Little Jesse James*. Occasionally a song from a musical would stay with him for a brief while, but his preference was for opera, particularly the Germans, and he loved drinking songs. He usually whistled one whose title seems to come out something like "Going to a Wedding at the Heurigen," which is a familiar German drinking tune.

In June 1934, Benchley scribbled on one of his programs, "A reviewer is only flesh and blood . . . I am still in love with the following actresses: Maude Adams, Florence Reed, Laura Hope Crews, Julia Marlowe,

Maxine Elliott, Ethel Barrymore, Janet Beecher, Ina
Claire, Jane Cowl, and Pauline Frederick."

December 1, 1934, was opening night for Lillian
Hellman's *The Children's Hour*. This predated *In Cold
Blood* by about thirty years, but it used the same
formula: a true-life criminal case reported with tech-
niques usually reserved for fiction. Most people thought
the play *was* fiction, and it's possible Miss Hellman may
not have appreciated the fact that Benchley brought up
the Drumsheugh matter in his *New Yorker* review. He
didn't include her among his favorite people, and it's
possible that he later blamed Lillian Hellman for Dorothy
Parker's new interest in left-wing causes. "They're such
*serious* girls," he once told a friend.

It is so much the fashion nowadays for critics to
boast in print about the books they've read that it's
almost staggering to readjust to somebody with genuine
modesty who thought it rather bad taste to name-drop
books, like so many love affairs. People were usually
surprised when it turned out that Benchley had read
almost everything. Certainly he was very much up on
the Drumsheugh affair.

It seems that in the year 1810 Edinburgh found itself
confronted with "a blazing scandal," according to
William Roughead. There was a school for young ladies
run by two gentlewomen, Miss Marianne Woods, who
was a niece of a famous actor, and Miss Jane Pirie, the
daughter of an Edinburgh writer. The school residence
at Drumsheugh was small and neither lady was a particularly good businesswoman. Miss Woods had an aunt

who was a Shakespearean player, just as is the case in *The Children's Hour*. A little girl named Jane Cummings was sent to Drumsheugh when she was eight years old. She was not a very nice little girl. She reported to her grandmother that the relations between Miss Woods and Miss Pirie were not always what they should be . . . a case of life imitating art-that-was-to-be.

Benchley noted that the criminal action in the play was one of libel, and pointed out that it should have been slander; he was probably right.

On December 29, 1934, Benchley remarked, "I used to say that I could laugh at Phil Baker and Lou Holtz till the cows came home. Well, the cows came home last Thursday night in *Calling All Stars* . . ."

He loved Tallulah Bankhead in a revival of *Rain* and he was highly respectful of Elisabeth Bergner and said that she needed no introduction—we were the ones to be introduced.

Early in 1935 he was one of the first to praise *Awake and Sing*, the play by Clifford Odets. Benchley loved it— said it was excellent.

For a revival of *The Green Pastures* he noted, "Let us hope it will not be five years before we see it again. We need it oftener than that."

As for a revival of *The Taming of the Shrew* with the Lunts, Benchley said, "Mr. Lunt made it so funny you forgot it was *The Taming of the Shrew*—which is the top in anodynes."

The thirties were wonderful years for the theater. It was still the time of Great Stars: in addition to the Lunts, there were Jane Cowl, Ethel Barrymore, Ina Claire, Walter Hampden, Leslie Howard, Fay Bainter, Paul Muni, Laurette Taylor, Otis Skinner, Philip Merivale, and Noël Coward to be seen and adored by everybody who could dig up fifty-five cents for the second balcony, or three-thirty for orchestra seats. There was a pharmaceutical heaven for the impoverished stage-struck—Gray's Drug Store, on 43rd Street and Broadway, which housed in its basement a ticket agency called Leblang's. Cut-rate seats were available here, and on Saturdays just before matinee time there wasn't breathing space; people were snapping up cancellations and wondering whether to trust the critics' opinions or choose the available fifty-five-centers.

There was no off-Broadway in those days. The theater section was in the West 40s, and the rush for cabs wasn't nearly so hectic (most theatergoers couldn't afford cabs, anyway). First nights meant evening dress— some theatrical managers insisted on it—and there were at least fifteen or twenty good plays to choose among. The theater was entertainment at the height of its importance, and New York was its center. The movies may have drawn more paying customers, but prestige was based on Broadway.

At the end of March 1935, the "Goings On About Town" page in *The New Yorker* listed the following theatrical offerings:

*Accent on Youth*, which has been endlessly revived

on stage and in movies; *Awake and Sing*, the Group Theater's splendid production of Clifford Odets' realistic drama; *The Bishop Misbehaves* with Walter Connolly; *The Black Pit*, The Theater Union's angry study of life in the coal fields; *The Children's Hour*; *Escape Me Never*, with the famous European star Elisabeth Bergner; *Fly Away Home*, a comedy with Thomas Mitchell; *The Green Pastures* in one of its frequent revivals; *Laburnum Grove* with Edmund Gwenn and Melville Cooper (an actor who happened to resemble Robert Benchley very closely); a repertory company of the Moscow Art Players in several Chekhov productions; *The Old Maid*, the Pulitzer Prize play of the year, with Judith Anderson and Helen Menken, adapted by Zoï Akine from Edith Wharton's novel; *Personal Appearance*, a comedy about Hollywood with Gladys George; *The Petrified Forest*, Robert Sherwood's dramatic hit starring Leslie Howard with a supporting player named Humphrey Bogart; *Petticoat Fever* ("with Dennis King in top form, if you don't mind top form"); *Post Road* with Lucile Watson; *Three Men on a Horse* (another perennial summer stock comedy); *Tobacco Road* with Henry Hull; and Eva Le Gallienne's *L'Aiglon*.

In the musical lists were Cole Porter's *Anything Goes* with William Gaxton, Ethel Merman and Victor Moore, *The Great Waltz*, *Revenge with Music*, and *Thumbs Up*. Most of the tunes they offered are still used as standards today.

Scheduled to open the last week in March was another Odets drama, *Waiting for Lefty*.

It was a glorious time to be a playwright, an actor, a director, a manager or a part of an audience. At its best, it was the theater in flower and fulfillment.

# CHAPTER THIRTEEN

# "It Was a Perfectly Good Racket"

Frederick Lewis Allen, Benchley's classmate and editor of *Harper's* magazine, was very fond of Benchley, in common with the rest of the world, but began, in the mid-thirties, to lose touch with him. "Bob is cordial," Allen remarked, "but tends to elude me . . ." He had some qualms at the time about Benchley and success, but he seems to be the only person who had even this slight reservation about Benchley. And there was no question about Allen's basic feeling for him. He said, "I've never had a friend who was nicer. He's proof that you don't have to be mean to be funny." But he remarked to his family, "Isn't it funny that this person, who is so admirable, is now so hard to know?"

Frederick Lewis Allen's son, Oliver, while at Harvard

during his senior year bumped into Robert Benchley
when Oliver was with his classmate, Robert Benchley,
Jr. Said the senior Benchley to Oliver, "Why, Freddie
Allen! I'd know you anywhere; you haven't changed a
bit."

One of the reasons for Benchley's absentmindedness
around this time of his life may have been Louise Gill
Macy Brown Hopkins Gates. When Benchley met her
she didn't have all those names; she had had only one
husband, Clyde Brown, of whom she had remarked,
"He's not theater people, he's private people."

Someone who remembers Louise Macy very well
said that "she was beauty and magic all in one—she was
an event." Louise Gill Macy was born in Pasadena, was
educated in the East at the exclusive Madeira School in
Greenway, Virginia, and had spent two years at Smith
College. She married Clyde Brown, Jr., February 28,
1932, and divorced him in Nevada on December 23 of
the same year. One friend of the family says that from
the very first night of their marriage it was clear that
nothing was going to work out.

Louise, called Louie, was tall; she had blue eyes, not-
quite dark brown hair and a clear-cut hairline. Taken
separately, her features didn't add up to conventional
beauty, but she seems to have bowled over everyone
with whom she came in contact.

Louise's older sister, Gertrude, was hired by Guthrie
McClintic, and went on to become Katharine Cornell's
personal manager. The sisters met a great many theater

people. Benchley reacted to Louise just about the same as everybody else: he found her irresistible.

A friend of Benchley's says that, at "21," the brightest table in the room would be that shared by Benchley, Louise, and often James Forrestal, who was to become Secretary of the Navy. Louise would be the only woman with them and always looked absolutely radiant. The Kriendlers claim that she was a true beauty; Tony Soma says that she wasn't nearly as good looking as Betty Starbuck. It's a matter that will probably never be settled.

Benchley would take Louise and Forrestal to his old haunt, Polly Adler's, after "21" closed. Louise called it slumming, and she was probably one of the few women of her particular background who was making the scene at Miss Adler's, even in a tourist capacity.

With her extreme chic, Louise had no trouble getting a job as fashion editor on *Harper's Bazaar*. She tended to wear a great deal of black, but her clothes were always young in feeling. She would wear a little sailor hat and a diamond pin; and her hems were a half-inch longer in back than in front to avoid what she called "the falling forward look." She had a first-rate fashion sense.

Clothes were changing in the early thirties. There was a return of normal waistlines and long skirts. Hats were worn outdoors by both men and women. The Paris dress models were too intricate to be copied unless the copies were very expensive themselves, and they were cut on the bias. Shoulders were padded into right-

angles, and ruffles drooled to the ground a la Ginger
Rogers, Carole Lombard, and Joan Crawford. There
wasn't as much mass market appeal as there is in today's
clothes, probably due to the cost of the detail. Evening
dresses were usually backless, which meant no underwear. Wealthy women began the custom—which still
obtains—of having undergarments made for each exclusive gown, skeleton structure, like the steel founda-
tion of a skyscraper.

Louise did well at her job. Not only Benchley and
Forrestal, but John Hay Whitney—who was by then
divorced from Liz Altemus, and not yet married to
Betsy Roosevelt—saw a lot of her. Whitney was fifteen
years younger than Benchley, and Louise was a few
years younger than Whitney. Whitney claims that it's
probably Louise who made up "Gramps" as a nickname
for Benchley.

Louise's formal education didn't make much of an
impression on her; she had a kind of innocent bright-
ness. When she saw Katharine Cornell in Chekhov's
*Three Sisters*, she said, "Oh, this is very interesting. Has
he written any other plays?" Benchley, the dedicated
reader, tried to influence her intellectual life. *He* usually
read four books at a time, with markers in each, but
Louise wasn't cut out for even one book at a time.

In 1938 Louise Macy took over the Paris office for
*Harper's Bazaar* and came back during the war, after
doing her part in helping refugees who had fled to
Paris for safety. For her work she was chosen god-

mother of a regiment of Americans who volunteered to fight for France.

She continued her war work when she came back to New York and was a member of one of the first Red Cross Nurses-Aid classes here. When Louise Macy was thirty-six years old she met Harry Hopkins, Franklin D. Roosevelt's closest adviser. For Hopkins, it was a case of desperate love at first sight.

Louise had special knotted-gold jewelry made for the Macy-Hopkins nuptials, which were held at the White House. Some of the guests were President and Mrs. Roosevelt, Robert Sherwood, and the Ludingtons. Benchley didn't attend, but the wedding fitted in with one of his bits of private philosophy: "I place my women well. . . ."

This referred not only to Benchley's women, really, but to everyone he took an interest in, such as Ricki Soma, the daughter of Benchley's good friend, Tony Soma. Ricki was about fourteen when Benchley supplied her theater tickets on condition that she write her own reviews of the plays. She grew up to be a magazine model, went to Hollywood, and married John Huston, the director. Their daughter, Anjelica Huston, is now an actress.

After the wedding, Louise moved into the White House with Harry Hopkins. Stricken with ulcers, Hopkins had to leave Washington. The couple came to New York and took an apartment on Fifth Avenue overlooking the Park, and, as Louise said, "also overlooking the rent." After Hopkins' death in 1946 of cancer Louise married Geoffrey Gates at the Ludingtons' in Ardmore, Pennsylvania. Gates was a New York architect who lived in Oyster Bay and managed Mill Pond House, an antique shop. Gates, too, died of cancer. Louise went on to run Mill Pond House herself, until her death in the 1960s.

One of the couples with whom Benchley and Louise Macy often dined was S. J. Perelman and his wife, Laura, the sister of Nathanael West. Benchley was a great admirer of Perelman, who was just beginning to be well-known. When Perelman's collection *Strictly from Hunger* appeared, Benchley provided a forword that served three purposes. It was kind to Perelman, it got in some digs at Max Eastman, who had written an analysis of humor—the kind of earnest nonsense Benchley deplored—and it praised Benchley's idol, Ring Lardner. The introduction to *Strictly from Hunger* is typical Benchley in many ways:

"Someone once said that writing an introduction to a book is like a pretty girl, but he escaped me before I could find out what he meant by it. I chased and chased him, but he was younger and quicker than I was, and so I never did learn the pay-off.

"From here the Nile flows in a northwesterly direction until it reaches the clam-flats, where it is intercepted by countless red and green posters reading '*Etat*,' meaning that the French government operates

the railroads. (This experiment, incidentally, has been
highly successful, as witness the white lace antimacas-
sars on the backs of the seats of the railway carriages
with the same word '*Etat*' embroidered on them.)
Here the lagoons become flowering fields and, as the
sun sets over the seed-grass, or oil-ducts, we see an
entirely different Nile, the Nile of Al-Kahar, of Chinese
Gordon, of Brickley, Mahan and Casey. Also, if one
were so minded, the hippopotamus gives way to the
smaller, but no less ruthless, dick-dick, and the tropical
rains begin.

"We can, I feel certain, base our assumption that
Swift was married to Stella (for an assumption it must
be until we have proven our point) on a letter recently
discovered by Heegy in the library of the Orthopedic
Church at Malmsley. Swift (the Gloomy Dean) was
acquainted with Stella. This we know. His preoccupa-
tion with vapors of one sort or another has been shown
in *A discourse Concerning the Automatic Operation of
the Spirit, Inspired on the Occasion of the Seventh
Birthday of Sir William Temple* ('89). LeBaudy's testimony confirms the other biographers, Raglan's in particular, and we are safe to assume that when he
wrote: 'I had te [the?] 100 lbs. in my Pocket' he
meant that he had already brought some sort of culmina-
tion to his relations with Stella, or Vanessa, as she was
later to be known.

"Somehow, I like Mrs. Ramm's translation of '*Io
son, cantava, io son dolce sirena*' better. Mrs. Ramm
gives it this: 'She sang: "I am the siren of sweet sound".'

"This, as I see it, has more of the mysterious vision which visited Dante, more of the Homeric completeness. You can just hear 'dem darkies strummin',' and, for pictorial effect, there is nothing more lovely than 'I kiss your little hand, Madame' for 'Ce n'est que votre main, Madame.' Or did I lose my place?

"But *how* shall we learn from experience? Call it empiricism, if you will, but empiricism what? James's answer is that we learn actively and not passively. Okeh. But is that all? James found in Hume an 'intolerable disintegration of experience.' That was all very well for James to say, but he later wrote to Holmes of his 'image of ideals being the vanishing points which give a kind of perspective to the chaos of events.' What kind of talk is this? There *must* be one thing or another, 'else what's a heathen for?'

"In conclusion, let me quote from the final plea to the jury of George D. Robinson, Esq., for the Defense:

"'So far as you are concerned, this is the last word of the defendant to you. Take it: take care of her as you have, and give us promptly your verdict of "not guilty," that she may go home and be Lizzie Borden of Fall River in that bloodstained and wrecked home where she has passed her life for so many years.'

*"If the reader (who shall be nameless) has detected a certain lack of cohesion in the preceding introduction to Mr. Perelman's book, it has been due to an equally certain desire on my part to confound Mr. Perelman as he has confounded me. For Mr. Perelman, and I*

*say it with rancor, nipped my writing career in the bud and drove me into movie-acting.*

*"Together with several others of my ilk, most of whom are now on movie relief, thanks to Mr. Perelman, I was making a decent living writing fugitive pieces for the magazines, pieces which, while not pretentious, we fondly imagined sprang from a congenital insanity which could be turned into thirty dollars here or forty dollars there. It was a perfectly good racket, at any rate, and several psychiatrists were good enough to refer to it as 'free association,' or Dope's Disease.*

*"Then, from the Baptist precincts of Brown University, wafted a cloud no bigger than a man's hams, which was S. J. Perelman. It consisted at first of little drawings with abominably hand-lettered legends, but it held a menace for all of us who were pretending to be insane for profit. Here was the real Magoo, a natural son of the Prophet Da-Da, and he was only an undergraduate.*

*"From then on, it was just a matter of time before Perelman took over the dementia praecox field and drove us all to writing articles on economics for* THE COMMENTATOR. *Any further attempts to garble thought-processes sounded like imitation-Perelman. He did to our weak little efforts at 'crazy stuff' what Benny Goodman has done to middle-period jazz. He swung it. To use a swing phrase, he took it 'out of the world.' And there he remains, all by himself.*

*"In the comprehensive index to Max Eastman's somewhat less than comprehensive analysis of* LAUGHTER,

*we find the following section in the list of names under*
*"P".*

Pegler, Westbrook
Penner, Joe
Perkins, Eli
Perl, R. E.
Phelps, William Lyon

*"The omission of 'Perelman, S. J.' from this par-*
*ticular book is not surprising, as he probably didn't*
*bother to answer Mr. Eastman's preliminary question-*
*naire on 'What Is Humor?' But if Ring Lardner had got*
*out a book on American Humor (which he most cer-*
*tainly would never have dreamed of doing), I'll bet*
*that 'Perelman, S. J.' would have led all the rest in that*
*particular field which Lardner himself loved the best.*

Robert Benchley"

# CHAPTER FOURTEEN

# "Fine —
# Just Hurting Inside"

As a father, Benchley was unfailingly kind and loving—when he was home. And he was, Gertrude Benchley has pointed out, around more than most people who knew him as a boulevardier were apt to realize. He wouldn't get many points for togetherness, if anybody was keeping score, but somehow he managed to win more affection and respect from his children than a good many fathers who spend most of their lives glueing airplane models together in the basement playroom.

Nevertheless, it wasn't until the late 1930s, according to Nathaniel Benchley, that he really got to know his father. Young Benchley was a married man by then and living in New York. With or without his wife he would often accompany his father on one of those

long evenings on the prowl. There was a great deal of
warmth and well-being between them, for Benchley,
Sr., made it clear that Nat was being chosen as a friend,
not a son.

A favorite daytime spot for the Benchleys was a little
section of Riverside Drive near Grant's Tomb where
there was a small gravestone with this epitaph:

*Erected to the memory of an Amiable Child*
*St. Claire Pollock*
*Died 15 July 1797*
*In the fifth year of his age*

Benchley loved this memorial—he took as much pride
in the gravestone as though he were a descendant of
St. Claire Pollock.

Grant's Tomb was the scene of a typical Benchley
incident. During the late '30s, Benchley had been at
a party given by friends on Riverside Drive. He left
and walked around by himself, ending up at the Tomb.
It happened that two of his friends were behind him,
but he didn't know that. The friends saw him pick
up something, write on a piece of paper, and then
put whatever it was back on the ground. When Benchley was gone, the friends drew near. There was an
empty milk bottle outside the tomb, now with a note
stuck inside it: *One milk, no cream, signed, U. S. Grant.*

In the fall of 1939, Robert Benchley went on the radio,
which in those days was the big entertainment medium
for the home audience.

Out of the wooden Gothic domes that housed the
Stromberg-Carlson or the Atwater Kent, the American public was listening to royal entertainment. Fred
Allen, one of the great comedians who enlivened Sundays with his special repertory company, Allen's Alley,
pointed out that radio was the best theater ever invented because it made people use their own imagina-
tions. It also made sponsors spend huge sums on the
best talent available: Jack Benny, Eddie Cantor, W. C.
Fields in combat with Charlie McCarthy, Colonel Stoop-
nagle and Budd, the Lux Radio Theater, Rudy Vallee's
weekly showcase for stars, Kate Smith, Bing Crosby,
Ed Wynn, and—most popular of all—Amos 'n' Andy.
Young performers often got their start on the Major
Bowes Amateur Hour, conducted by the Major himself in a curiously bad-tempered, querulous voice; and
the Horn & Hardart Children's Hour, Let's Pretend,
Little Orphan Annie, or Jack Armstrong delighted the
in-school set.

A show that starred a comic would usually back
him up with a name band, a vocalist, and a series of
short episodes in which the comic's particular traits
(Benny's stinginess, Allen's cynicism, or Robert Benchley's engaging helplessness) were exploited.

The Old Gold Show starring Robert Benchley ran
from the fall of 1939 through the spring of 1940. Benchley didn't write his own material, but he was himself;
so it was a funny show. He had his own little stock
company for five-minute skits and the orchestra was
led by young Artie Shaw, who was very much the

radical in those days. In fact, Artie Shaw would try to get Benchley to discuss Marxist economic systems, realizing that Benchley was an Established Intellectual.

"I can't even keep my check book balanced," Robert would say kindly.

Del Sharbutt was the announcer on the show, and would often accompany Benchley on his rounds until 4 A.M., but they would always show up on time for rehearsal the next morning at ten. After rehearsal Robert would take Del to "a sanctuary of sorts" (which turned out to be the Harvard Club) and would pass his friends breezily, saying in answer to the usual how-are-yous, "fine, just hurting inside," with an aside to Sharbutt, "Class of 1903." Usually they reached a small hidden bar with two booths and two brandy milk punches waiting for them through some sort of radar signal.

Benchley loved to have people tell him stories, and Del Sharbutt cheerfully accommodated. Benchley still persisted on with his belief that he himself couldn't possibly tell a joke with the skill, for example, of Bob Hope, whose technique, Benchley thought, worked equally well with "first, second and third level gags."

Before every weekly broadcast, Benchley would come out to "warm up the audience" and naturally the most logical thing for him to do was *The Treasurer's Report*. He would bring along his Noah bag, carried under one arm as though it were a woman's handbag. Pulling out an assortment of unrelated, absurd objects, he would eventually wave the script of *The*

*Treasurer's Report.* Every week he put different odd-
ments (an alarm clock, a Harvard pennant) in the Noah
bag, mainly for the purpose of breaking up the cast
of the show. *He* was tired of *The Treasurer's Report*,
but the audience adored it.

Sharbutt convinced him that it would be a good
idea to brace himself with just one double brandy
before doing the report. It wouldn't be enough to affect
his speech, and it would make him feel better.

"You know, you're right. I'll go right into the act
that way," said Benchley, beaming. And it seemed to
work. Benchley was fond of Sharbutt and loved to hear
about the old days at the Paramount when Del played
the organ. Occasionally, Del would go through his
repertoire of *Abide With Me, I Come to the Garden
Alone,* and *Rock of Ages,* which pleased Robert very
much.

There were guest stars on the show, including Jimmy
Durante. He was an old friend of Benchley, who used
to worry that Durante would be embarrassed by some
of the rehearsal scripts in which long words appeared.
Benchley would want to have the words changed—
all unknown to Durante, of course.

There was a fussy little account executive who visited
the show during rehearsals, making sure everyone was
smoking Old Gold cigarettes. He wore spats, was always half-drunk and red-faced and sat with folded
arms during the rehearsals. Benchley would greet the
little man with a nervous, polite laugh; it was the laugh

he always gave to people he really didn't care very much about.

At the time of the radio show Benchley hired a new secretary. She can be referred to as Jenksie, her real name being quite a mouthful. One legend has it that Jenksie was without a past and arrived at the Royalton by parcel post. A most unreliable source claims that one day Benchley's radio broke; a repair-man came to fix it, brought Jenksie along with him, and somehow she became a fixture, too. But a soberer informant has it that Jenksie was the daughter of a Pittsburgh steel worker. The family was desperately poor and, out of necessity, Jenksie learned to be an excellent short-order cook. Her childhood was not particularly happy, and one Christmas, as she told it, her stocking contained nothing but a lump of coal . . . (This would have touched Benchley as much as the story some people insisted on—that Jenksie was brought up in an orphanage.) In any case, she seems to have had a succession of jobs, among them hatcheck girl and script girl at M-G-M. This may have been where she really met Benchley; it is a fact that she filed the scripts of the Benchley shorts and even played a bit part in one.

Benchley was captivated by a remark of Jenksie's early in their acquaintance. They were at a party, and the talk had reached a temporary lull. Suddenly Jenksie got up and said, "Sniff. Sniff. Somebody in this room has brown eyes."

Benchley was no one's idea of a slave driver. At the radio show rehearsals he would say to Jenksie, "Where do you suppose that note is?" She'd say, "I think I know." He'd say, "Oh, I would be so grateful if you'd find it."

Often when they were alone Benchley and Jenksie would listen to Methodist hymns on the phonograph. They had no satirical intention; they really enjoyed them. When they weren't playing Methodist hymns, they played a lot of gin rummy. At one point, somebody figured out that Jenksie owed Benchley $7,000,000.

Jenksie was not the world's best secretary. Once she asked, "What does a secretary do?" She was told vaguely that a secretary made lists of things for her employer. Jenksie asked Benchley: "Would you remind me to make a list?" "Yes," he said, "when?" And Jenksie responded like any Katherine Gibbs girl: "Now?"

She was a remarkably sweet-faced person with big gray eyes and brown hair, quite slim and with a fey quality. She was not at all pretentious. In fact, when a friend of Benchley asked, making polite conversation: "What do you do?", Jenksie replied, "Well, I'm supposed to be a secretary, but I've got a blouse-full of goodies."

Ann Honeycutt, the writer, was one of Benchley's cronies. She knew most of the interesting people in town and turned up practically everywhere. When Benchley took her to "21" the first time Ann was new in the city and wasn't very sure what to order. Benchley ordered them each a martini and some melon-and-ham.

When Ann had another martini, she thought she should ask for another portion of melon-and-ham, and so it went through three or four. Benchley said, "Well, get a good thing and stick with it." After lunch Benchley hired a limousine and took Ann to a milliner's where she was having a hat made. When she came out of the shop, she found her escort sound asleep in the corner of the Cadillac. The melon-and-ham had gone to his head.

One day Ann, with her friends, Dorothy Parker and Dawn Powell, decided to pay a call on Mr. Benchley, as Mrs. Parker still called him when she wasn't calling him "Fred." On this particular day he *was* being called Fred. The ladies put off their visit to old Fred until they had fortified themselves at "21," which took, as Ann remembers, about six hours. (The service must have been slow that day.) Well-fueled, the ladies visited Fred in his room at the Royalton where they discussed issues of importance, such as Miss Powell's recent encounter with a stuffy young British author who had said he wanted to bring his bicycle here.

"Do bicycles have any special privileges in America?" he asked Miss Powell.

Miss Powell considered. "Well, they can't vote," she pointed out reasonably.

The ladies were bound for the theater, but Miss Powell left one of her white cotton gloves behind. "Fred" stuffed it with Kleenex and hung it on a wire stretched at five feet above the ground in front of his window curtains. Somehow the ladies made it back from the theater, having refreshed themselves further, and reported on the play to Benchley. They said it was a terrible play. They said the acting was awful. They said they couldn't hear anything. They said the sets were dreary. The production, they concluded, was a mess.

Benchley studied them for a moment and said, "Well, I always think you get much more out of the theater if you sit facing the stage."

Roland Young once told a friend that Benchley's niceness consisted in equal parts of empathy, compassion and guilt, and that Bob was the only person in the world who could keep writing about himself "without tipping his hand."

One of the people Roland Young and Benchley used to take to dinner was a girl called simply The Professor. Her place of employment was Polly Adler's where, for her usual assignments, she wore only pince-nez glasses. Her appearance with Young and Benchley during the early evening in well-known restaurants gave them a great deal of academic satisfaction.

When the radio show ended in the spring of 1940, the cast decided to give Benchley a surprise party. Unfortunately, it was too much of a surprise; they waited until the last minute to ask Benchley to drop in casually at the Sharbutt's. By that time Benchley had another engagement and when he found out about the reason for the festivities, he was remorseful. He wrote Sharbutt a note that he sent along with one of the Mark Cross Noah bags. The note said: "This is a very odd-looking bag, used for old rye bottles, half-filled packages of cigarettes and extra door keys. I'm sure you will find great use for it . . . the average man wouldn't. P.S. I'm sorry I missed your party."

The rest of the cast got Noah bags, too. Benchley could never resist spending money at any time, for any reason.

# CHAPTER FIFTEEN

# "It Might Make One in Love with Death"

P. G. Wodehouse once said to a friend: "Bob Benchley said I mustn't believe the stories that I had heard
about the ill treatment of inmates at Hollywood studios,
for there is little actual brutality. Most of the big
executives are kindly men and Bob has often seen Louis
B. Mayer step outside some nodder's hutch and push
a piece of lettuce through the bars. A nodder, of course,
is slightly lower on the social scale than a Yes-man. After a conference when the Yes-men had finished speaking, the nodders nod. There is also a sub-species known
as nodder's assistants, but that gets too technical. And
it isn't true that they are all lunatics in Hollywood.
Bob knows fully half a dozen people who are practically
sane, except of course at the time of the full moon."

Hollywood *was* a madhouse. Dominating the dreams of a depression-conscious America it was presided over by a handful of monarchs whose beginnings had been in the garment industry. The producers were the real stars, although what the public saw were the much prettier faces of Loretta Young or Robert Taylor and the rest—Louis B. Mayer and the Warner Brothers never were seen outside of their palatial offices. The studios themselves looked like outdoor factories, and the factory product was the opium of depression children. For ten or fifteen cents, you could sit all afternoon watching beautiful actors disporting themselves in exquisitely appointed penthouses (interior decorators flown out especially at $3000 a week to be "technical advisers") or lavish country houses. Bad economic times didn't affect Hollywood, except to insure its success—people spent money for movies when there wasn't enough to eat in the house; man—luckily for M-G-M and Paramount—didn't live by bread alone.

When a laborer was earning about six dollars a week in the late 1930s, Garbo was pulling down about $9000. Hollywood Boulevard, the center of this demented universe, along which every beauty contest winner walked hopefully, was called Mammary Lane by the more cynical inhabitants of Beverly Hills, the residential section of fake-Tudor and Mediterranean palaces. The stars employed Cordon Bleu cooks in their homes but ate daily at the studio commissaries—if they worked for Louis B. Mayer they ate chicken soup free at lunch—and arrived for work at 5 A.M. after what the public liked to think of as Roman orgies—more likely evenings spent watching re-runs of old successes that would yield tips on flattering camera angles.

The year 1939 was a good one for the dream-factory. Motion Picture Industry United States Box Office receipts that year were $659,000,000.

Hollywood in the 1930s saw a mass importation of authors from all over the world. Aldous Huxley found himself next door to an ex-pulp-magazine writer. William Faulkner, brought to Hollywood on an astronomical salary, stayed on without ever really finding out who most of the screen stars and directors were. For a while, Mrs. Parker also went along for the ride, and, among other chores, contributed the lyrics to "I Wished on the Moon," which was used in one of the *Big Broadcast* movies. The song referred to an April day that wouldn't dance away, and offended nobody. On the rebound, Mrs. Parker wrote for *The New Yorker* what Benchley considered to be her funniest short story. It was called "Mrs. Hofstadter on Josephine Street," and it dealt with Mrs. Parker's own life in Hollywood with her husband, Alan Campbell, and a black servant who happened to be a snob. The idea of making fun of a black bothered Mrs. Parker later and she never allowed this story to be anthologized. In fact, she didn't even like people to refer to it, which is a pity.

From the time Benchley made his first film short, *The Treasurer's Report*, his commutation from East to West Coast became more and more burdensome. Unwillingly, Benchley had to hand in his resignation as

*New Yorker* drama critic in order to keep up with his film schedule.

He took an apartment at the Garden of Allah ("squat palms and pink stucco") because he said he was enchanted by the idea of mail arriving for him at the Garden of Allah, Hollywood. This was a collection of hotel bungalows around a swimming pool, built by the Russian actress Alla Nazimova. There had already been a successful movie and novel called *The Garden of Allah*, so she allowed the gods their final "h." One next door neighbor was Benchley's old friend, Marc Connelly. On the other side was Charles Butterworth, a Protestant leprechaun who was born in South Bend, Indiana, and appeared in a number of Broadway shows before he decided to make Hollywood his career. He was a small man, with a dedicated vacuity of expression.

One day Benchley and Butterworth attended a tennis tournament at a girls' nudist camp at the edge of the desert. They watched the ladies serving and lobbing for awhile, then Butterworth turned to Benchley with his usual complete lack of emotion and said, "Who's ahead?"

Benchley led rather languorous and leisurely days at the Garden of Allah, although when he was working he had to be on the set quite early in the morning. Once he told Marc Connelly that he had been very much annoyed when his alarm clock had gone off right in the middle of a game he was watching between "the Incas and the Uncas." When the bell sounded, Benchley mumbled, "I've just got time to hear the rest of this," but he couldn't get back to sleep so he never did discover how the dramatic match came out.

His non-dream life also had its disappointments. For Benchley the Boulevardier, Hollywood was tame stuff. He complained of it this way:

". . . with high excitement I made my first trip to Hollywood, the Sin Capital of the World. 'Here it comes at last!' I giggled to myself. 'Life in the raw, and then down, down, down!' I could hardly wait. I shall never forget my first night in Hollywood. I had taken a room at a hotel, and with me was Marc Connelly, a tea merchant who had knocked around the world a bit, and Charles Butterworth, a romantic actor of that period. We had dined wisely, but not very well and were in the mood for about three-quarters of an orgy.

"Mr. Butterworth said that he knew a beautiful girl that he could call up. 'We'll have a million laughs,' he said. A million laughs wasn't my idea of what constituted a Hollywood orgy but I figured out that everyone didn't necessarily have to laugh all the time.

"He called the phone number of the beautiful girl, and while he was waiting he reassured us again. 'She's the most beautiful girl you ever saw,' he said. Then, after a long wait, he added, 'She's so beautiful, she isn't even home!'

"While Charlie called some other actresses' numbers, Marc and I tried to see who could recall the oldest popular song. It was great fun! Then, all of Charlie's numbers either being out or on the point of

going to bed, we hit upon a great plan for the rest of
the evening.

" 'Let's go over to Henry's and get an egg sandwich!'
said Marc. Like a flash we were off and ten o'clock
saw us in the middle of our second egg sandwich,
washed down with an equal number of beakers of
milk. Henry's was the only place in Hollywood that
stayed open after 9:30, so we were in great good luck
to find it.

". . . I met lots of movie actors and actresses eventually, but I guess I got into the wrong set, because
they were all crazy about tennis and early rising. The
nearest I got to temptation was once when I went
out of the movie colony to Santa Barbara to be best
man at Donald Ogden Stewart's wedding and got water
on the knee. But I did that all by myself, nobody
tempted me.

"Sometimes now I think of those quiet evenings in
Hollywood under the reading lamp and wonder if it
wouldn't be better if I had stayed there among the
orange juice."

People close to Benchley claim that he really wasn't
happy in Hollywood. The manners and mores didn't
please that New England conscience: sitting around a
swimming pool in the warm sunshine was not Benchley's idea of how to contribute to the eventual good
of mankind. In fact, the only time he ever had cross
words with Nathaniel and his wife was in Hollywood
when Marjorie Benchley said she would love to bring
up her children in the pleasant surroundings of the

Garden of Allah. Benchley lost his temper and told her to stay away from Hollywood and all it stood for.

Benchley may also have been suffering another pang of conscience. For several years he had found it more and more difficult to write. Those wonderful effortless pieces that seemed to flow endlessly from the center of his being were not really that easy . . .

Still, there were good times at the Garden of Allah. There was, for example, the horse that Benchley owned, together with John McClain. McClain had been staying with him at the Garden of Allah. At a Hollywood track they ran into Whitney and a couple of his horses. One of these was called Sharpie, and McClain and Benchley decided to buy him. They joined the California Racing Association and selected colors and silks. The colors were rather unusual, a mixture of crimson for Harvard, brown for McClain and blue for Whitney-and-Yale. The program listed Sharpie as belonging to the Garden of Allah Stud Farms. On the day of the race, Benchley and McClain drove a rented limousine to the track, took one look at the silks and the jockey (resembling a mad stained-glass collage) and McClain had a very logical foreboding of calamity.

"Suppose he doesn't win?"

"That's all right," said Benchley. "Sharpie can have my bedroom and I'll sleep on the couch in the living room."

But Sharpie won his race, paid four to one, and was claimed. To celebrate the occasion, "21" added a new little jockey to the line-up of statues on their outside steps for Benchley and McClain.

*Dancing Lady* was one of the endless cycle of backstage movies in which Ruby Keeler and/or Joan Crawford (lowly understudies) stepped into the star's shoes and became an overnight sensation. In this one, Franchot Tone, repeating his true-life role as a playboy fascinated by the theater, undertook to improve Miss Crawford's social tone: "Don't say 'skip it'," he commanded her. "The correct phrase is 'drop it'." And it was his duty to inform her that refined ladies didn't wear bows on their shoes. Clark Gable was a tough backstage dance director, and Benchley was his drunk confidant. Movie after movie, Benchley became *everybody's* drunk confidant. He began to weary after a while, as he did the same thing again and again in: *Ann Vickers, Rafter Romance, Social Register, China Seas* (with Gable and Harlow), *Piccadilly Jim* and *Broadway Melody of 1938.*

For a man who started out in Worcester, Massachusetts as a social worker, this was all very embarrassing.

In 1940 Benchley not only acted in, but contributed to, the script for *Foreign Correspondent*, for Alfred Hitchcock. During the making of this movie, he arrived on the set one day, perhaps a little more tired than usual, but smiling that smile that crinkled his eyes.

Hitchcock took one look at him and said, "Bob, *open* those naughty little eyes!"

In 1940 a movie called *Hired Wife* with Rosalind Russell and Brian Aherne showed Bob as a kind of chaperone—and—family-lawyer, who sang "Little Brown Jug" and saw that the plot complications came out in the usual way. In *Take a Letter, Darling*, directed by Mitchell Leisen in 1942, Rosalind Russell and Fred Mac-Murray had some sort of business relationship. Mac-Murray had just been offered a job for $50 a week, which made someone in the film say quite sincerely (it *was* 1942), "Lucky stiff!"

Benchley played confidant and adviser to Rosalind Russell who, as usual, was successful, brilliant, and beautiful. Of one man in the film, Benchley remarked, "He hates all women except his sister—he just dislikes her a lot." Benchley didn't have a great deal to do with the all-over quality of the script, however—unfortunately. In a love scene between MacMurray and Russell, Miss Russell announced: "If I ever fall in love, it will be the sea dashing against rocks!" Small wonder Benchley wouldn't open those naughty little eyes.

Then there was *Nice Girl* with Deanna Durbin, *The Reluctant Dragon*, made by Disney (which Benchley found untrue to the Kenneth Grahame story), and *You'll Never Get Rich* with Benchley's old friend, Fred Astaire. (They had worked together before, in 1927. Benchley had written the book for the Gershwin show, *Funny Face*, starring Fred and Adele Astaire.) Then followed *The Major and the Minor*, *The Sky's the Limit*, and *Song of Russia* for M-G-M in 1943. It was while making this film that Benchley, wearing some sort of Russian garb out to lunch, met an old friend on the street who asked, "What are you doing here?"

"I'm a shill for Shostakovich," said Benchley.

To celebrate Robert Benchley, Jr.'s, twenty-first birthday, Benchley interrupted a movie and crossed the continent to be with his family. Back in Hollywood, he called Gertrude because he had forgotten something. "You know," he told her, "I really love that island." He meant Nantucket, of course, where he wanted Gertrude to buy a cemetery lot. He had quoted the preface to Shelley's eulogy on the death of Keats: "It might make one in love with death to think that one should be buried in so sweet a place." This was *not* a premonition of his own death; it was simply Benchley expressing a wish that had always been with him.

Benchley often quarreled with the management at the Garden of Allah. Once he was trying to call Gertrude and he couldn't rouse the switchboard operator. He went into the lobby and proceeded to turn all the furniture upside down. He left a note for the sleeping switchboard girl: "Let this be a lesson to you. I might have been having a baby."

In 1940 he was ill with pneumonia, and his Hollywood doctor gave him one of the new sulfa drugs.

Benchley took his pills, and then he and Charles Butterworth decided to show the American Medical Association just how miraculous these drugs really were.
Before the doctor's visit, Butterworth and Benchley
opened a down pillow and, with great care and a little
glue, attached the feathers from the pillow all over
Benchley from waist to toes.

When the doctor arrived, Benchley was lying in bed
with the covers drawn up just under his shoulders.

"Do you notice any effect from the sulfa?" asked
the doctor.

"No," said Benchley. "I'm sorry, but it really didn't
seem to have any effect on me at all."

"That's funny," said the doctor. "This stuff's supposed to be so wonderful . . ."

Benchley said he couldn't help that. Nothing at all
had happened. The doctor put on his hat and prepared
to leave.

"Wait a minute," said Benchley. "There is just one
little thing . . ." And he threw back the covers and
showed the doctor the feathers.

Benchley would still commute to New York now and
then, and on one of his visits an old friend telephoned
him about some tickets for a mystery play.

"I'll take you to a Broadway opening," said the
friend.

"Oh, is that where people go and dress up and exchange smart talk? I've always wanted to go to one
of those," said the former drama critic of *Life* and

*The New Yorker*. He and his friend met at "21." Bob
had already had a long afternoon and, when they got
to the theater, he fell asleep in his seat. Suddenly a
telephone rang on stage. Benchley awoke and shouted,
"Will somebody please answer that phone!" Then he
added, "I think it's for me."

The play wasn't much good anyway, and the next
day one of the reviews read, "Show terrible but Benchley superb in small part."

When a friend of Benchley's arrived in Hollywood
on a visit, Bob said he wanted to take her on a tour.
Jenksie was with him at this time. They took their
New York visitor on the Benchley Hollywood Glam-
our Tour. It consisted of a visit to the May Company
store, a view of the garage where Thelma Todd died,
the Pacific Ocean, and Dave Chasen's restaurant. To
conclude the tour, they passed a ravine into which
Benchley shouted *"Chloe!"* at the top of his voice.

Later in the evening, dining at Romanoff's (Benchley's West Coast "21"), the group spotted Amos and
Andy sitting at a nearby table. Their radio program
had just begun to slip. Benchley thought they might be
depressed and went over to them with a long story beginning, "I am a strange man pretending to be Robert
Benchley . . ." and kept them amused for the rest of
the evening.

During the making of one of his movies in which
some penguins appeared, Benchley said that he was
beginning to go a little soft, not on all birds, but just
penguins. He was beginning to lose some of his deep

bird-hate. In fact, when he read that the penguins in a
British zoo were looking unhappy, he took up their
case at once. He claimed to have received a cable from
a penguin which read: NOT REALLY UNHAPPY BUT JUST
BLUE STOP HEAR OF PENGUIN SHORTAGE IN HOLLYWOOD
STOP WOULD THERE BE OPENING FOR A YOUNGSTER WHO
BIDS FAIR TO BE SECOND SHIRLEY TEMPLE? SIGNED BLACK-
FOOT BERT.

As though penguins weren't trouble enough, somebody on a "little" magazine approached Benchley for
a definition of humor. Still obsessed with his dream
of doing away with all analyses of humor forever,
Benchley replied, "I can only tell you what Schwanzleben said in his work, *Humor After Death*. He hits on
this point indirectly when he writes, 'All laughter is
a muscular rigidity spasmodically relieved by involuntary
twitching.' "

At the Brown Derby in Beverly Hills, Benchley, Marc
Connelly, Charles Butterworth, Harry Ruby the song-
writer and a few others formed an Athletic Club. Since
the sport that interested most of the members was
going to nightclubs and drinking, the club never achieved
national dimensions.

Someone accused Butterworth of embezzling the club
funds, which made him so angry he resigned. It was
promptly renamed the Stay-As-Sweet-As-You-Are-
Athletic-Club.

There was a path around the swimming pool between Benchley's villa and Marc Connelly's. One Sun-

day morning Marc saw his friend arriving rather early for Benchley-on-a-Sunday.

"Why, Bobby, what are you doing here?" asked Marc.

"I just had an argument with M-G-M," said Benchley. "They seemed to think I was intoxicated on a set but I have proof that this isn't true. Luckily, I had the presence of mind to have a photograph taken—they were doing a shot with a highball glass in my hand. See how clear it all is—you can see the ice made of cellophane . . . and my hand as steady as a rock."

But Marc noticed that where Benchley's head should have been on the photograph was a dim cloud . . .

# CHAPTER SIXTEEN

# "Go to a Place
# Where There Is Laughter"

Paying a visit to put flowers on Edmund's grave at West Point, Jennie Benchley once remarked to a cadet:

"I'm the daughter of a soldier, the widow of a soldier, the mother of a soldier, but thank God I'll never be the grandmother of a soldier."

She was wrong to a degree, for in 1943 Nathaniel Benchley went into the Navy. Robert, Jr., was working in the Norden Bombsight Plant near New York, and Robert Sr. kept up his commutation from Hollywood to New York with a bit more emphasis on New York now that he had a son within hailing distance.

Benchley invited Robert, Jr. to move in with him at the Royalton. There was only one bed, but that didn't present much of a problem. Benchley, Sr. would busy himself all night cultivating agreeable strangers at bars and at 6 A.M. he would return to the Royalton, shake Bob, Jr. and say, "My turn in the bed."

One of Benchley's companions on these nocturnal rounds remembers that they often ended up at the Stork Club, where the owner—in his own cups—would slowly and thoughtfully pour champagne on Benchley's head. But on one occasion, Benchley's companion was deserted suddenly in a taxi, because they caught sight of a cop beating a black. Benchley went along to the police station to see that justice was done.

The more he acted in movies and the more the years crept over him like wee red ants, the harder it became for him to write. Finally, in December, 1943, when Benchley was fifty-four, he made a farewell announcement. He said he was through with writing and that he was going to devote the rest of his time to the movies.

The New York *Herald Tribune* ran an editorial about it:

"Many of our writers, once regarded as excellent humorists, live to a great age under the amiable but often pathetic illusion that their powers to create laughs are in no way diminished with the passing years. They are not critical enough to be bored with themselves. Mr. Benchley may be wrong, but his example is salutary."

Of course he *was* wrong. The pieces stand up today as very little else of the humor of the '20s and '30s does. He could never get over the feeling, though, that

he was something less than many of his famous friends
who had gone on to win Pulitzer Prizes and critical
acclaim. Once he groaned to a friend, "Look at me—
a clown, a comic, a cheap gagman. There's a career
for you."

"But what did you want to be, Bob?"

"I wanted to be a Social Service worker and I
wanted to write a history of the Queen Anne period."

In talking about the renunciation of his magazine
pieces, Benchley would say, "No, I haven't written anything in a long time. When I did write a piece, I
would rewrite it, then polish it; it took a lot of time,
and then I'd find out that Thurber did it better fifteen
years before." But then, Thurber had said the same
thing about Benchley.

The commuting from coast to coast continued. One
author, very much indebted to Benchley, saw a good
bit of him on both coasts. At a Hollywood party the
author needed to use a bathroom, but decided instead
on a corner of the elaborately-furnished living room.
Benchley looked at him, turned away and walked into
another room. The next morning the author conva-
lesced from an epic hangover and went into total
remorse. Instead of sending a dozen long-stemmed roses
to his hostess he sent them to Benchley. Benchley received the roses, understood their import and telephoned his friend. "John," he said, "there is no need to
apologize to me. *I'm* your friend, and all your friends
*know* you're a son of a bitch."

There seemed to be something about Hollywood parties that brought out the dark side of a guest. Even the affable Benchley was no exception. There was the embarrassing occasion at which his friends, Dorothy Parker, Scott Fitzgerald, Robert Sherwood and others were in attendance. Sherwood had just received another Pulitzer Prize, and Fitzgerald was beginning to receive serious critical acclaim.

Suddenly Benchley said to no one in particular, "Those eyes—I can't stand those eyes looking at me!"

People stopped talking and stared at Benchley, who was now backing away from Sherwood. Everybody thought it was a joke; but it wasn't. Benchley pointed at Sherwood and said, "He's looking at me and thinking how he knew me when I was going to be a great writer and he's thinking *now* look what I am!"

This scene was probably the only one of its kind that ever took place. Benchley was seldom introspective and almost never said anything that indicated the slightest amount of self-pity.

In 1953, S. J. Perelman—who felt much the same about this sort of thing as Benchley—appeared at a college conference where he was called upon to discuss "The Nature of Humor." "Someone far more eloquent than myself," he said, "could write one of those 11,000 word essays for a little magazine inquiring why it is that although people sob unashamedly at soap operas, they rarely have the courage of their laughter. When I used to work for the Marx Brothers a couple of decades ago, it was no uncommon experience to see

moviegoers emerge from their pictures (tears of pleasure still streaking down their cheeks), take a deep sober-
ing breath, and observe uncomfortably, "My, wasn't
that silly?"

In the spring of 1945, Nathaniel Benchley was transferred to duty in the Pacific, and he and his wife spent
a week at the Garden of Allah with Robert. There
was an evening when they went to one nightclub
after another, then finally back to the Garden of Allah
where Benchley, Sr. said, "I like it better here with
just us. You know, the only reason I used to take you
out and around to all those places was so that when
you couldn't afford to do it on your own, you'd
realize that you weren't missing anything." This was a
rather ironic observation coming from the man who
had probably been seen around town more than anybody of his era.

Among the last pictures Benchley made were
*Duffy's Tavern*, for Paramount, *Road to Utopia*, with
Bing Crosby and Bob Hope—the same Bob Hope whom
Benchley admired so much as a technician ("if he would
only get rid of that blue material"), and *Weekend at
the Waldorf*. In 1945 he made a movie short called
*I'm a Civilian Here Myself*, about demobilization, for
the United States Navy. Later on, Benchley's friend,
James Forrestal, Secretary of the Navy, asked to have
it.

Sometime in October 1945, Benchley had a thorough
physical check-up while he was on the West Coast.

Everything was fine; in fact, he remarked of the laboratory report on his stool: "It could be used for party favors."

That November, Benchley was back in New York at the Royalton. The weekend of the 17th, when Robert, Jr. was with him, Benchley had a nosebleed that wouldn't stop. A cab and a doctor were summoned (Benchley's regular doctor was out of town). He was taken to a private hospital and later transferred to the Columbia-Presbyterian Medical Center. Somehow the doctors failed to give him an anti-coagulant in time; it had been assumed that the proper steps had already been taken. The impossible happened: on November 21, 1945 Robert Benchley died of a cerebral hemorrhage.

The physical check-up on the coast was accurate enough; Benchley had had a surprisingly strong constitution. His reflexes were amazing. He had been able to outwrestle his son, Nathaniel (although he said, "I save my energy for times I might need it"), so his last illness came as a gigantic shock to people who assumed that that exquisitely structured personality would go on forever.

If all Benchley's friends had attended his funeral there wouldn't have been a chapel in the world large enough. What actually took place was a very private service: Gertrude, Nathaniel and his wife, Robert, Jr. and his wife, and one house guest, at a crematorium at Ferncliff in Westchester. Then the ashes, placed in a

Noah bag, were taken to the beloved island at Nantucket. The gravestone there said simply,

1889 – 1945

—Robert Benchley

the name appearing after a small dash in the manner
of the famous *New Yorker* signatures. That time of
his life had been a happy one for Benchley, and he
would have appreciated his son Nathaniel's thoughtful-
ness in arranging the epitaph. When Harold Ross heard
about it his eyes filled with tears.

Long before, when George Ade died, Robert had
taken the news sorrowfully. He said then, "When a
great humorist dies, everybody should go to a place
where there is laughter and drink to his memory until
the lights go out."

Robert's friends decided to honor him in exactly the
way he would have wished. There were two separate
wakes held, one in New York at "21" presided over
by Marc Connelly, and the other at Romanoff's in
Beverly Hills, presided over by Dorothy Parker.
(Mrs. Parker had taken over Benchley's lease at the
Garden of Allah.)

For the occasion, Gertrude Benchley donated stills
from the Benchley movies for wall decor at "21." Most
of Bob's friends came, although Roland Young wouldn't
accept the invitation because he thought the whole
idea was in bad taste.

John Hay Whitney remembers the wake at "21":
"I was there . . . we drank many healths and refrained
from sadness . . ." One of the toasts was Marc Con-

nelly's. It took note of the time-difference between
the ceremony at Romanoff's and the ceremony in New
York, and it went, "To Bob—there was no such thing
as time in loving Bob . . ."

Someone else said, "After this, heaven will have to
keep open after hours—" and Thurber asked, "But who
will listen to our troubles now that Bob is gone?"
Donald Ogden Stewart replied, "Just put a letter in
the mail, like letters to Santa Claus. It will get there."
The evening wore on and on, and if memories of it
are dim, that was just what Benchley would have
wanted.

It was almost impossible for people to realize that
Benchley was gone. He had always been there, whenever he was needed. As a confidant, as a flawless companion, as everybody's childhood fantasy of a "best
friend," Benchley had always been most things to most
men. Mrs. Benchley received letters and tributes from
so many people that one large scrapbook couldn't con-
tain them.

November 21 had been a great blow to a great many
people. Life was never the same for anyone who had
ever spent even a few hours with the epitome of the
verray parfit gentil knight.

Some of Benchley's colleagues, who were completely
overcome, could only begin to sum up what he had
meant to them. Wolcott Gibbs, who succeeded Benchley as drama critic of *The New Yorker*, wrote: "People
were mysteriously improved in his company on a level
of easy charm of which no one would have dreamed

he was capable." Frank Sullivan said, "I find myself
getting my admiration for Bench's work mixed up with
my affection for him. I had a wholesome, benign envy
of Bob. I just wished I could be as comical as he was.
I also wished I could be the social person he was,
sought after by one and all." Donald Ogden Stewart
said, "He *was* humor with its instinctive humanity,
toleration, wisdom, non-competitiveness . . ."

Along with the sincere, heartfelt tributes came a few
odd memoranda. Several years after Robert's death,
Gertrude received a newsy letter from Jenksie, who
had married, settled down and had just given birth to
a baby boy. Her idea was that she would name the
child for Robert and Mrs. Benchley could pay the
boy's way through school.

At the end of November 1945, Gertrude received
a letter from one of the restaurants Benchley had preferred. Her lawyer remarked, "Oh, how nice, they're
sending you a condolence note"; but it wasn't. It was a
bill in four figures, covering years of drinks for many
people, celebrated and otherwise.

It might have embarrassed Benchley if he'd known that
three of his friends praised him in rather historical
terms. Patricia Collinge remembered him as having the
greatest sense of justice of anyone she'd ever met; John
Hay Whitney said Benchley was "the dearest man I
have ever known," and Howard Dietz called him the
wisest.

This was the sum of something written centuries

before, and it isn't altogether presumptuous to recall Plato's words on the death of Socrates, in *Phaedo:*

"Such was the end of our friend, concerning whom I may truly say that of all men of his time whom I have known, he was the wisest and justest and best."

*Posthumous collections.

1929   Lesson No. 1 (Fox)
1929   Stewed, Fried & Boiled (Fox)
1929   Furnace Trouble (Fox)
1933   Your Technocracy and Mine (RKO)
1935   How to Sleep (M-G-M)
1936   How to Behave (M-G-M)
1936   How to Train a Dog (M-G-M)
1936   How to Vote (M-G-M)
1936   How to Be a Detective (M-G-M)
1937   The Romance of Digestion (M-G-M)
1937   How to Start the Day (M-G-M)
1937   A Night at the Movies (M-G-M)
1938   How to Figure Income Tax (M-G-M)
1938   Music Made Simple (M-G-M)
1938   An Evening Alone (M-G-M)
1938   How to Raise a Baby (M-G-M)
1938   The Courtship of the Newt (M-G-M)
1938   How to Read (M-G-M)
1938   How to Watch Football (M-G-M)
1938   The Opening Day (M-G-M)
1938   Mental Poise (M-G-M)
1939   How to Sub-Let (M-G-M)
1939   An Hour for Lunch (M-G-M)
1939   Dark Magic (M-G-M)
1939   Home Early (M-G-M)
1939   How to Eat (M-G-M)
1939   The Day of Rest (M-G-M)
1939   See Your Doctor (M-G-M)
1940   Inferiority Complex (M-G-M)
1940   Home Movies (M-G-M)
1940   The Trouble with Husbands (Paramount)
1941   Waiting for Baby (Paramount)

1941  Crime Control (Paramount)
1941  The Forgotten Man (Paramount)
1941  How to Take a Vacation (Paramount)
1942  Nothing But Nerves (Paramount)
1942  The Witness (Paramount)
1942  Keeping in Shape (Paramount)
1942  The Man's Angle (Paramount)
1943  My Tomato (M-G-M)
1943  No News Is Good News (M-G-M)
1944  Important Business (M-G-M)
1944  Why, Daddy? (M-G-M)
1945  I'm a Civilian Here Myself (U. S. Navy)

# INDEX